INDIAN HISTORICAL STUDIES

Photo by the Archæological Survey of India] THE SANCHI STUPA

[*Frontispiece.*

INDIAN
HISTORICAL STUDIES

H. G. RAWLINSON

WITH 7 ILLUSTRATIONS AND MAP

GYAN

Published by

GYAN

Gyan Publishing House
5, Ansari Road
Daryaganj, New Delhi-110002
Phone: 011-47034999, 9811692060
E-mail: books@gyanbooks.com

Distribution Network
gyanbooks.com
India, USA, Canada, UK, Australia, France

ISBN : 9788121236072 (PB)
First Published, London, 1913

2nd Impression 2020

Printed at: Gyan Press, Delhi.

Indian Historical Studies
Author: H. G. Rawlinson

INDIAN
HISTORICAL STUDIES

BY

H. G. RAWLINSON, M.A.

LATE SCHOLAR, EMMANUEL COLLEGE, CAMBRIDGE; PROFESSOR OF ENGLISH LITERATURE, THE DECCAN COLLEGE, POONA

AUTHOR OF "BACTRIA: THE HISTORY OF A FORGOTTEN EMPIRE"

WITH 7 ILLUSTRATIONS AND A MAP

LONGMANS, GREEN, AND CO.

39 PATERNOSTER ROW, LONDON

NEW YORK, BOMBAY, AND CALCUTTA

1913

Truth is One,
And in all lands beneath the sun,
Whoso hath eyes to see may see
The tokens of its unity.

"Truth is one: the wise name it variously."

Rigveda, I. 164. 46.

PREFACE

I HAVE to thank the editor of the *Times of India* for permission to reprint the paper on Ibn Batuta and part of that on the Chinese Pilgrims; the managing committee of the *Bombay Branch of the Royal Asiatic Society* for similar permission with regard to that on Foreign Influences in the Civilization of Ancient India; the Archæological Department of the Government of India for the photographs of the Indo-Greek Buddha, the Sanchi Stupa, and the Asoka Pillar; and Dr. A. K. Coomaraswamy for the exquisite *Prajnâpâramitâ*—one of the most beautiful pieces of statuary in the world. The map accompanying the volume is the work of Mr. Bhidé of the Agricultural College, Poona, who executed his task with great care and skill.

INTRODUCTION

Few people, either in England or in India, take any real interest in Indian History. Englishmen are repelled by the remoteness and strangeness of the theme; and the vast majority of Indians, up to very recent times, have regarded the subject with indifference. History plays no part in the traditional Sanskrit curriculum. It was left to Western scholars to decipher the inscriptions of Asoka, and to rescue from oblivion the caves of Ellura and the Ajanta frescoes. Orientalists, however, have usually made the great mistake of treating the history of præ-Mahommedan India almost exclusively from the archæological point of view. Ancient Indian art is regarded as a curiosity rather than as a triumph of artistic achievement; and the political organization of the empire of the Maurya or Gupta monarchs is seldom accorded the admiration it deserves.[1] India still awaits a historian who will not be satisfied with date and names, but will make the early history of the country *live;* who will not content himself with recording dry facts in their proper sequence, but will duly estimate the artistic, literary, and political achievements of successive dynasties.

[1] Indian writers err in the other direction. From a mistaken sense of patriotism, they generally consider it their duty to praise their country at all costs, and in so doing, invariably defeat their own ends.

It is a lamentable fact that under the system in vogue at most Indian Universities, the student knows more of Julius Cæsar or the battle of Marathon than of Chandragupta or the teaching of Gautama. We employ lecturers to instruct our pupils in western ethics; but we forget to encourage them to study the admirable "sermons in stone" of their own emperor Asoka, written as they were for the edification of the people at large. No student should be allowed to waste his time over Greek and Roman history, while remaining ignorant of what the Greek historians and the Chinese travellers have to tell him of his own country and her past. Another work which we urgently require is a "source book" of early Indian History, containing translations from the various authors, Greek, Chinese, and Indian—including, of course, the inscriptions—of all passages bearing upon early Indian History. The passages, with explanatory notes, arranged in their chronological order, would form an admirable text-book for history students. From the Greek and Latin point of view, something of the kind has been done by McCrindle,[1] while for the Mahommedan period we have the excellent work of Elliot and Dowson.[2] The study of Indian history on the lines I have indicated might, perhaps, do something to arrest the appalling decay of taste which is one of the saddest features of modern India. It might also check, in England and America, the spread of rubbishy ideas, propagated under the title of Oriental philosophy, by charlatans who often cannot read a

[1] *Ancient India as described in Classical Literature*, by J. W. McCrindle.

[2] *The History of India as told by her own Historians*, 1867.

line of Sanskrit. This nonsensical pseudo-Orientalism has done more than anything else to alienate serious people, and to deter them from studying the really great civilization and literature of the East.

The studies which are here offered to the public do not form in any way a continuous series. The author has, however, attempted to give the reader a glimpse of India in nearly every epoch of her history by taking a leading figure of the period and attempting an estimate of his achievements. The study of Buddhism and its founder is largely founded on Oldenberg's great work, *Buddha, sein Leben, seine Lehre, und Seine Gemeinde*, of which a new edition appeared in 1906. Warren's *Buddhism in Translations* (1896) gives the original passages in an admirable fashion; and Dr. Rhys Davids' *Vinaya Texts* and *Dialogues of the Buddha* have been freely used. For Asoka we have the accurate, but not very inspiring, translation of the Edicts by Mr. Vincent Smith, to which the author is much indebted, though he has felt justified in making his own translation where necessary. Those who wish to know more about the Indo-Greek princes are referred to the author's *Bactria: the History of a Forgotten Empire* (Probsthain, 1913). Most of us have to depend upon the specialist as regards Chinese. For the Chinese pilgrims the translations of Beal (Trübner, 1884) Watters, [1] and the early work of Julien, are the most generally useful. The travels of that jovial Moor, Ibn Batuta, replete with interest for the student of early Mahommedan India, were first completely translated by Défrèmery and Sanguinetti (4 vols., 1858), though a rare book, Lee's

[1] *Oriental Translation Fund*, xiv., xv.

translation (1823), of an imperfect manuscript in the Cambridge library, may be occasionally met with. Much sentimental nonsense has been written about Akbar; the student is advised to consult the *Akbar Nama* of Abul Fazl and form his own opinions. It has been partly translated by Gladwin (1783), and Blockmann (1848). The best-written history of the whole Mahommedan period is Keen's *Short History of Hindustan;* Colonel Malleson's *Akbar*, in the "Rulers of India" series, is not very clearly arranged. The story of Shivaji is to be found, by those unacquainted with Marathi, in Grant Duff's *History of the Mahrattas.* The writer had access to many documents now lost, but it is a pity he adopts a consistently hostile attitude to the great guerilla leader. On the other hand, Justice Ranadé's *Rise of the Maratha Power* (Bombay, 1900) is disfigured by extravagant laudation of his hero's political achievements. The story of Robert Knox may be found in his autobiography, a famous book in its day, which may have even inspired the author of *Robinson Crusoe.* It has been recently edited by Mr. Ryan from fresh documents discovered in the Bodleian by the late Mr. Daniel Ferguson. To Indian readers the account given by Knox, of Ceylon, is of unique interest. In that island, undisturbed by Brahminical reaction or Mahommedan invader, survived a Buddhist community practically unchanged since the mission of Asoka in the third century B.C. What Knox says about the Sinhalese trade-guilds is especially important. The story of Ranjit Singh and of the Sikh nation may be found at greater length in the admirable works of Sir Lepel Griffin and in the exhaustive treatise of the late

Mr. Macauliffe. It is hoped that these brief studies will serve to stimulate the reader to a deeper study of a fascinating and neglected subject, of vital importance to all who are concerned with the oldest and noblest appanage of the Crown.

H. G. RAWLINSON.

BURWASH,
SUSSEX, 1913.

CONTENTS

LIST OF ILLUSTRATIONS

I

GAUTAMA BUDDHA.

I

GAUTAMA BUDDHA.

Λέγει που Ἡράκλειτος ὅτι πάντα χωρεῖ καὶ οὐδὲν μένει.

THE sixth century B.C. was destined to be a momentous one in the history of the Aryan races. Northern Europe, it is true, was still plunged in darkness, and even in Italy only remote signs of the dawning of a new era were perceptible. But further east a general awakening was setting in. Greece was in a state of ferment. Greek colonists were supplanting the Phœnicians all along the shores of the Mediterranean; in Hellas itself, old political institutions were breaking down on every hand, and old beliefs were being rudely questioned. In Western Asia, the great Semitic empires of the Euphrates valley were beginning to totter before the rising power of the Iranians. In India, too, indications of an impending revolution were not wanting. A great change had come over the robust nomads who had poured through the passes into the Panjab some two thousand years previously. As they spread further to the east, they lost a good deal of the simplicity and vigour which had characterized them at first. The enervating climate of the Ganges valley was partly responsible for this; contact with the aboriginal races and absorption of their ideas had also had considerable effect. The involved philosophical speculations of the Upanishads had succeeded the primitive nature-worship of the Vedic hymns; caste distinctions had begun to draw rigid barriers between class and class.

At this crisis, probably about 568 B.C., Gautama Buddha was born. His father was a petty chieftain who dwelt on the borders of Nepal. His very name (Suddhodana, Clean Rice) indicates that the ancestral wealth of the family was derived from the fertile rice fields on the borders of the Rohini, a little stream which watered the lands of the tribe on its way to join the Ganges. In all probability his clan, the Sakyas, was not originally Aryan at all, but an offshoot of one of those hordes of Sakas or Scythians who were constantly finding their way into India from the Central Asian steppes. But early India was not discriminating. The Sakyas, like the Rajputs at a later date, soon forgot their Scythian origin, and became incorporated in the Hindu polity as members of the Warrior Caste. Perhaps it was to this touch of foreign blood that Gautama owed his peculiarly vigorous temperament.

Gautama was an only son, born when his parents were advanced in years and had almost despaired of offspring. He was born in a wayside garden, since immortalized by pious Buddhists,[1] while his mother, following the immemorial custom of the East, was on her way to her parents' home to await her delivery. She did not long survive his birth, and this circumstance made the child doubly precious in the eyes of his widowed father. We need not here concern ourselves with the host of legends—some exquisitely

[1] It was marked by a pillar erected by Asoka, and recently discovered.

Gautama Buddha.
From an Indo-Greek Statue.
(*By permission of the Director-General of Archæology.*)

[*To face page* 5.

beautiful, others merely grotesque—which have grown up round the birth and boyhood of Gautama. Some resemble so strangely the stories related of the birth and childhood of Jesus Christ, that we may only suppose that they were borrowed, centuries later, from the Nestorian Church of Southern India, or from the semi-Christian sects of Persia and Asia Minor. Others, such as the legend of the "Bending of the Bow," are attached in some form or other to every Aryan hero. All we can tell for certain is that Gautama was brought up as an ordinary prince of the period, and in due time was married and begot a son. Then, at about the age of twenty-one, came the turning point of his career.

The life of a man was, according to the ancient Hindu rule, divided into four stages. After fulfilling the duties of the student and the householder, he was free, if he so desired, to abandon the world, and to retire with his family to a forest hermitage, there to spend his days in pious exercises. Finally, if he succeeded in snapping the last links of attachment to things of earth, the hermit might become a mendicant, and wander forth in rags and poverty to beg his food from door to door, unrecognized even by his kin. This idea of a peaceful sunset following the storms and turmoils of life has always exercised a peculiar fascination upon the Hindu mind, for in India both the climate and the charitable disposition of the people render the hardships of such an existence far less trying than they would be in the West. Even in our own days, a distinguished statesman has abandoned fame, wealth, and ambition for the forsaken, homeless existence of the *Sanyasi*.

This idea appears to have presented itself very early to the mind of Gautama. His father, anxious to hand on his kingdom to his only son, tried his best to divert him from such thoughts. Elaborate precautions were taken to shield the young prince from the sight of anything disquieting: such allurements as the little court could offer were lavishly employed to captivate and distract his mind. These devices, however, had precisely the opposite effect to that which the originators of the scheme had intended. Gautama had long been wearied by the aimlessness of his petty round of pleasures: instead of attracting, they repelled and disgusted him. In the words of the old chronicler, he realized that the "Householder's life is full of hindrance, beset with passion; but the homeless life is as free as that of the bird on the wing." An accident crystallized these vague feelings into a definite resolve. One day, while driving through the streets of Kapila-Vastu, his eye fell upon a sight common enough in the East—a beggar lying by the roadside, crippled and disfigured by a loathsome disease. "Are there many like this?" he asked of Channa, his charioteer. The reply was in the affirmative. Gautama's mind was quickly made up. His duty as a householder, according to Hindu ethical standards, was fulfilled: he had a son to take his place, and he was free to depart. He resolved to go forth and seek some solution to the secret of all this pain and suffering. And so, a few nights afterwards, he bade a silent farewell to his wife and son, and crept out of the palace. Calling the faithful Channa, he bade him saddle the horse Kantaka, and the pair rode out into the darkness together. Just as dawn was breaking, he dismounted, discarded his rich robes, cut off his long hair, and sent home his attendant to break the news to his family. Then, clothed in sorry rags, the erstwhile prince set forth upon the quest. At first he attached himself to the renowned teacher Alara, whose disciples dwelt in a hermitage among the caves near Rajagriha. From Alara he went in despair to Udraka, another famous philosopher, but philosophy afforded no practical solution to the questions he sought to answer. The image of the dying beggar in the streets of Kapila-Vastu still haunted him. Five of Udraka's disciples, however, had decided to try whether by penances and austerities they might not gain that supernatural insight which was said to be obtained by these methods. To these Gautama attached himself, and for six years he practised such frightful self-torture that his fame as an ascetic rang through the land, in the words of the Pali commentator, "like the sound of a great bell hung in the heavens." So exhausted was he by the long course of penance that one day he fainted while bathing in a stream, and would have probably died had not a herdsman's daughter revived him with a draught of milk. But the promised insight never came: he was as far off from the long-sought-for solution as ever. And now Gautama took a characteristically bold resolve. Abandoning his austerities, he returned to ordinary life, and determined to start afresh. At the sight of his apostasy, his former friends turned their backs upon him, and he was left utterly alone. But the end was nearer than Gautama imagined. Seated that night under a gigantic pipal tree, he began to reflect upon the events of the past seven years: the vaunted Yoga of the Brahmin had proved a hollow fraud; was every attempt to prove the Everlasting Secret doomed to equal failure? Had he left wife and kingdom in pursuit of a phantom of the imagination? All at once, as he pondered, the long-sought revelation dawned upon the thinker's mind. The flash of intuition, which has come to the earnest seeker after the truth in many ages and nations, which we call Conversion, and the Indians Enlightenment or Buddhi, broke suddenly upon Gautama with a final answer to all his perplexities.

The clue to the secret of existence, as conceived by Gautama, was, strangely enough, even then upon the lips of the philosopher Heraclitus in the West. "Nothing is permanent," was the fundamental tenet of both philosophers.

> "The hills are shadows, and they flow
> From form to form, and nothing stands;
> They melt like mists, the solid lands,
> Like clouds they shape themselves and go."

All is transitory, the earth beneath our feet, the starry heaven above us, the gods, and, above all, that ever-varying complex of emotions which men call Personality or Soul. The cause of suffering is ignorance. Unable to realize the impermanence of things, men grasp at shadows—wealth, honours, sensual satisfaction—as if they were realities. So, too, they shun decay, death, material losses, as if these were real disasters, and not what the Stoics called 'Αδιάφορα, things indifferent and inevitable. Man, then, has no soul, in the sense in which the word was generally understood both in Gautama's days and our own. The personality is only the concrete result of the propensities, which are modified at every moment of our existence by some stimulus from without. Gautama, however, did not discard the old belief in transmigration, which had taken such a deep hold upon the Hindu imagination; for transmigration provided a scheme of inevitable justice, whereby every action, good or bad, brings its own reward or punishment upon the doer. At death we pass into nothingness, even as we came, "dust to dust and ashes to ashes," according to the eternal law of synthesis and dissolution. But, in some mysterious way, the passions which we have generated, the desires which we have nurtured, have acquired a separate being, and, being liberated by the dissolution of the personality, find for themselves a new life in which to satiate their thirst for existence. And so every action of ours is determining the destiny of a future life for good or ill. *Vitaï lampada tradunt.*

The paradox of transmigration without a transmigrating soul was never explained satisfactorily by Gautama. He insisted on our belief in it, but forbad, with equal insistence, speculation upon so fruitless a subject. Later commentators have striven to explain the meaning by analogies from nature. If we plant a mango in the earth, the tree which springs up is the same, yet not the same, as the fruit which was planted; the flame, springing from one lighted lamp to another, is the same yet not the same as the first flame. "That which thou sowest thou sowest not that body which shall be, but bare grain, it may chance of wheat or of some other grain." And yet, so indissolubly is the latter life involved in the former, that Gautama himself often spoke in a loose fashion of his former lives, or his actions in a past birth.

In this system, it will be observed, there is no mention of God, of prayer, of remission of sin. The inexorable creed of Gautama found no room for these things. "As thou sowest, so shalt thou reap." Gods there might be—Gautama offered no opinion upon a matter so indifferent to salvation—but they, too, though perhaps more happy, powerful, long-lived than ourselves, are subject in the end to the same inevitable law. Like the gods of Epicurus, they take no part in earthly things; all our prayers and sacrifices are but

"Like a tale of little meaning, though the words be strong."[1]

What, then, is the end and object of life? The end, said Gautama, is Knowledge; for Knowledge is Deliverance. The wise man "puts away childish things": he ceases to yearn for worthless, transitory objects of desire.[2] And so, after a long series of transmitted lives, the thirst for existence is quenched; the oil in the lamp, to use a favourite Buddhist metaphor, is exhausted. The blissful day dawns when the man realizes that desire is dead within him—that the last links binding him to earth are snapped. This is Nirvana, "the quenching of the thirst." A little while he lingers on, pervaded by the rapt consciousness of final attainment; when he passes away, no-cravings survive to call a fresh life into being.

[1] Gautama appears to imply a belief in "gods," *dei* or *devas*, but he says nothing of "God," *Deus* or *Ishwara*. Gautama regarded the Unknowable very much as Herbert Spencer does.

[2] He has no desires, and so he leaves nothing behind him to find a fresh incarnation. The ideally wise man has killed all desire.

Buddhism has often been termed pessimistic. Nothing could really be further from the truth. Buddhism is essentially a cheerful religion. No Christian description of the delights of heaven could be more joyous than the outbursts of exultation over the happiness of him who has obtained Nirvana. Just as the sage in the great poem of Lucretius looks down upon the world as one on a cliff gazes upon the toilers in the raging sea below, the Buddhist saint

> "Looks down on the vain world and careworn crowd
> As he who stands upon a mountain-top
> Watching, serene himself, the toilers in the plain."

Charity is essentially a Buddhist, as it is a Christian, virtue, and Buddhism applies it, not only to suffering humanity, struggling in the meshes of desire, but to the animal world as well. The duty of compassion extends to all life, and Buddhism put a stop to the cruel sacrifices then common all over India. "Love your enemies" is another commandment common to Buddhist and Christian ethics. "Mine enemy has slandered, beaten, robbed, or abused me; whoso dwells upon these thoughts is never free from hate. Hatred ceases not by hate; by love it ceases. This is the ancient Law." "Oh, Joy! we live in bliss, hated, yet hating not again, healthy among the sick of soul." "To cease from wrong-doing; to get virtue; to cleanse one's own heart; this is the creed of all the Buddhas." Such exquisite sentiments are found scattered broadcast among the teachings of Gautama and his followers. Asoka fitly sums up Buddhist ethics in the following beautiful words: "What is the Dhamma? To eschew evil and follow after good, to be loving, true, pure of life, and patient, this is the Dhamma." This, then, was the "Noble, eight-fold path," as conceived by Gautama as he meditated beneath the Tree of Knowledge. It was a "Middle Path," avoiding the gloomy austerities of the ascetic. Above all, it was altruistic. Desire was to be forgotten chiefly by allowing our thoughts to dwell entirely upon others; the selfish methods of the hermit, who devotes himself exclusively to saving his own soul only, were utterly repudiated. Altruism is the distinguishing mark of Buddhism. It is said that while Gautama sat beneath the Bodhi Tree, the demons assailed him with numberless temptations; the subtlest was the constant prompting to enter into Nirvana forthwith, and leave the world to take care of itself. The temptation was real enough, though the demons were only the phantoms of an excited brain. But Gautama sternly put it away from him, and, girding up his loins, went forth upon his mission of preaching to mankind the great secret of life which had so marvellously dawned upon him.

His first thought was to go to Benares, a spot sanctified by immemorial tradition as the holiest centre of Hindu faith, and to commence his career as a teacher there. As he was laboriously toiling along the long road from Gaya to Benares, he met a Jaina monk, who was so struck by the "majestic light which shone in his face," that he asked him who the teacher could be who had conferred such bliss upon him. "I have no teacher," replied Gautama. "Of myself I have found Nirvana, and I go to Benares to kindle the Lamp of Life for those that sit in the valley of the shadow." "Are you the Jaina, the Conqueror?" said the monk. "Yea," replied

Gautama, "I am the Jaina, for I have conquered Sin and Death." Arrived at Benares, Gautama repaired to the Deer Park, a pleasant spot, shaded by gigantic trees, beneath which pilgrims were often to be found, meditating or resting. Here he encountered his late associates, the five ascetics. At first they welcomed coldly the supposed apostate, but awestruck by something in his appearance which told of the great change within, they were constrained to offer him the kindly acts of hospitality which are always shown to strangers in the East—to wash his feet and set food before him. Buddha then preached to them his first sermon. He was no longer Gautama, he said, but Buddha, and he showed them the true way of salvation. Thus the "wheel of the Law was set rolling" in the Deer Park at Benares. The five ascetics were the first converts, and they were quickly followed by a young nobleman of Benares named Yasha, and the three brothers Kasyapa, who had been worshippers of the Sacred Fire. The fires that really matter, said Buddha to them, are the triple fires of lust, ignorance, and hatred, and they must be quenched, not worshipped.

Converts now began to flock in numbers to the new creed. The conversion of Bimbisara, King of Magadha, was a signal triumph; more important, from a deeper point of view, was the acquisition of the learned and saintly Maha Kasyapa, who edited the Buddhist Canon after the Master's death. But Buddha made no distinctions of caste, wealth, or fame. Among his followers were Brahmins, kings, acrobats, barbers, courtezans, and reclaimed bandits; for all alike felt the winning influence of his strangely attractive personality. Of the many affecting and beautiful episodes of his life, none is more moving than the story of his return to the wife and family from whom he had silently parted so many years ago. It is said that he was at first received coldly, as one who had disgraced his lineage; but the sight of his son, standing begging-bowl in hand at the palace gate, was too much for the old rajah, who led him gently within and welcomed him with due honour. Poor Yasodhara, the wife whom he had abandoned, fell weeping at the feet of her long-lost husband; and Rajula, his little son, asked, "Father, give me mine inheritance." "My child," replied the Master, "Seek not the wealth that perishes: the inheritance I give to you is a seven-fold richer wealth, which I obtained under the Bodhi Tree." Rajula was received into the order as a novice, and many of the family followed suit. Among them was Ananda, Buddha's cousin, who became the Master's beloved disciple, accompanying him ceaselessly from henceforth to his death. Like Jesus Christ, Buddha is said to have formed an inner ring of twelve disciples, his constant companions and associates. Of these Ananda was the chief, though he was distinguished by qualities of the heart rather than the head. On the other hand, the signal success of the order created a host of bitter enemies and detractors, of whom Devadatta, another cousin of Buddha's, was the leader. The many attempts made to assassinate him, or to ruin his reputation by charges of murder or immorality, failed ignominiously, as they deserved to.

And now began the public ministry of Buddha, during the course of which he travelled for nearly half a century up and down the country, from Allahabad to Gaya, and from Gaya to the borders of Nepal. The sight of the little band of yellow-robed preachers soon became a familiar one in the villages of North-Eastern India, and the kindly teacher and his followers were eagerly welcomed. The Master, however, often preferred to lodge in the pleasant mango-groves outside the towns; and thither, when the heat of the day was over, the country folk would resort, and listen respectfully while a homely allegory, or folk-story, made to serve a moral purpose, was expounded. Like Jesus Christ, Buddha loved to instruct his hearers by means of parables drawn from the natural objects which they saw before them. Thus a forest-fire suggested a discourse upon the triple fire of desire. To a ploughman he remarked that he, too, was a husbandman; for faith was the seed which he sowed, and mindfulness the ploughshare. "And by my ploughing the tares of delusion are destroyed: sorrow is ended, and the blessed fruit of Nirvana springs up." Miracles of any kind Buddha never claimed to work. He told his disciples on more than one occasion that the true miracle is to convert a man by teaching: one who is merely attracted by magic is no true believer. On another occasion, we read, a woman of the name of Kisagotami came to him and implored him to restore her dead son to life. She was told that her son would be cured, if she brought a handful of mustard-seed from a house where none had lost parent, husband, child, or friend. From door to door the distracted mother went, but alas! in every family she found that death had done his deadly work. And so in despair she returned to the Master, who pointed out to her how inevitable, how universal is the law that all which is born is doomed to perish, and how fruitless are our strivings against the common destiny of material things. Pity for the afflicted was mingled with a kindly humour. "Master," said Ananda, "how are we to behave towards women?" "Look the other way, Ananda." "But if we can't avoid seeing them?" "Don't speak to them." "But if they speak to us, what are we to do?" "Keep a good look-out, Ananda; keep a guard upon your lips!" When a certain philosopher came to "prove him with hard questions," the Master sat silent, apparently absorbed in meditation. He maintained this irritating attitude till the would-be questioner went away in despair. Answering a remonstrance of Ananda as to the discourtesy of this behaviour, he pointed out that this was the only way to deal with such people. Nothing annoyed Buddha more than the endless metaphysical speculation which has been a perennial source of delight to the Hindu mind, to the detriment of practical religion. "I am not one of those teachers who teach an inner and an outer doctrine," he said; "I do not teach with the closed hand, concealing any mystery from the vulgar." The Esoteric Buddhism of some modern pseudo-Orientalists is a figment of the imagination.[1]

A life-like picture has been preserved for us by one of the commentators of how the Master spent the day. He arose at dawn, and out of consideration for his servant, dressed without assistance. Then he

[1] We must beware of confounding the teachings of Gautama with the mystical speculations of the later Mahayana Buddhists. This is a fruitful source of error.

sat down and meditated till the time came to go upon his rounds, when he donned his yellow robes, and taking up his begging-bowl, went round the town or village begging for alms. Perhaps some one would ask him to come and share the family meal; if so, he would sit down and eat with them, and after the meal was done, he would discourse to the assembly upon spiritual subjects, in a manner suited to the capacity of his audience. Then, returning home, he would wait upon the verandah till all had finished their repast, when he would assemble the disciples and suggest subjects for meditation. All would then disperse to rest and meditate. When the heat of the day was over, the folk of the neighbouring villages often came with presents of flowers and fruit and suchlike humble offerings, and the Master would preach them a sermon in a manner suitable to their beliefs. Then the Master used to bathe and await his disciples, who would gradually assemble when their meditations were over. Religious discourse occupied the time till the first watch of the night, when all retired. The Master slept lightly, and before it was light he often arose, and "calling to his mind the folk of the world, he would consider the aspirations they had formed in their previous births, and think over the means by which he could help them to attain thereto." In the rainy season, however, this nomadic life was impossible. The part of India where Gautama lived and taught is deluged by storms from June to October; heavy mists come down from the Himalayas, and the village roads become a quagmire. During this season the disciples repaired to one of the numerous retreats which had been presented to them, such as the bamboo-grove of King Bimbisara or the mansion of Ambapali, where they occupied themselves with study until the skies cleared and the dawning of the beautiful Indian winter called them forth once more to their work.

Time passed, and advancing years had begun to leave their mark upon the Master. In the fifty-first year of his ministry, a sharp attack of dysentery warned him that the end was near. He was now eighty, and the exposure and continued strain of half a century of teaching had left its mark. Calling his disciples together, he spoke to them long and earnestly of the greatness of the task which would fall upon them to fulfil after his decease. "My age is accomplished, my life is done; leaving you, I depart, having relied on myself alone. Be earnest, O mendicants, thoughtful and pure! Steadfast in resolve, keep watch over your own hearts! Whosoever shall adhere steadfastly to the Law and the Order, shall cross the Ocean of Life and come to the end of all sorrow." At the close of the rainy season, Buddha set out on his last pilgrimage. Arriving at the village of Pava, he became the guest of a poor smith, Chunda by name, who prepared a humble meal of boar's flesh, rice and cakes, to greet him.[1] The boar's flesh was evidently tainted; the Master, however, unwilling to disappoint his host, partook of the dish, excusing his disciples from doing likewise by a tactful hint that

[1] There is no need to explain away the term "boar's flesh." Gautama was not a vegetarian. Like Christ, he came "eating and drinking." The rule that he imposed upon his disciples was that no animal should be killed *in their presence or especially for their benefit.* That was all. Later refinements were due to Brahminical influence.

what was left over should be buried, as none but he could assimilate it. When the meal was over, the little party again took the road, but they had only gone a short way when the Master was seized with another violent attack of dysentery. However, he partly recovered, and proceeded slowly to the banks of the stream Kakuttha, where he bathed and drank, and appeared to be somewhat better. With his usual thoughtfulness, he sent back a message to Chunda by Ananda, telling him not to grieve because of the ill effects of his hospitable action. After this the Master journeyed a little further, but on reaching a grove of sala trees outside the town of Kusinara, he collapsed. Here there was a kind of rural couch or summer-house, and here, under the shade, Ananda spread a robe and laid his friend down to rest. It was noted that the sala trees were all in blossom, though the rains were over, and a peculiar kind of glow radiated, as the disciples imagined, from the body of their teacher. To their agitated minds it seemed as if the air were full of spirits; and some of them wept, but the wiser kept silence, for they knew that such things must be. The night wore on, and the Master talked long and earnestly about his approaching departure, till Ananda, overcome at the thought of losing his friend and companion of over forty years, went to the door of the summer-house and burst into tears. Buddha sent a disciple to recall him, and addressed him in words of infinite kindness and comfort. "Enough, Ananda: do not be troubled. How often have I not told you that all that we love must one day leave us? For all things that are born must also die: and whatever comes into being must also pass out of being. For many years, Ananda, you have been kind and good and faithful, very near to me by acts of love unvarying and boundless beyond measure. Be earnest, and you shall be free anon from the Four Evils—Individuality, Delusion, Sensuality, and Ignorance." And turning to the disciples, he praised Ananda's piety, faithfulness, and gentle disposition. A mendicant named Subhaddha came soon after to ask certain questions about the rival sects and their respective points of excellence. Ananda tried to turn him away on the plea that the Master was too ill to see any one; but Buddha called him in, and instead of answering his query, preached the Law to him, and received him as a convert into the Order. This was the last conversion made by the Master himself. The end was now near. Buddha said a few more earnest words about the Order and the duties of those who were henceforth to be responsible for its propagation, warning them to be lamps unto themselves, and to carry on the work. Then there was a long silence. In the third watch of the night the Teacher suddenly roused himself, and said with great and solemn emphasis, "Behold now, brethren, I exhort you, saying, Decay is inherent in all component things! Work out your salvation with diligence!" Saying this, he sank into a trance, from which he slowly passed, as dawn was breaking over the Himalayas, "Into that utter passing-away which leaves nothing whatsoever to return."

And so died one of the noblest and loftiest teachers that the world has ever seen.

II

ASOKA MAURYA, BUDDHIST EMPEROR OF INDIA.

II

ASOKA MAURYA, BUDDHIST EMPEROR OF INDIA.

272–231 B.C.

Εἰ τοίνυν ἄκροις εἰς φιλοσοφίαν πόλεώς τις ἀνάγκη ἐπιμεληθῆναι ἢ γέγονεν ἐν τῷ ἀπείρῳ τῷ παρεληλυθότι χρόνῳ ἢ καὶ νῦν ἔστιν ἔν τινι βαρβάρῳ τόπῳ, πόρρω που ἐκτὸς ὄντι τῆς ἡμετέρας ἐπόψεως ἢ καὶ ἔπειτα γενήσεται, περὶ τούτου ἕτοιμοι τῷ λόγῳ διαμάχεσθαι, ὡς γέγονεν ἡ εἰρημένη πολιτεία καὶ ἔστι καὶ γενήσεταί γε, ὅταν αὕτη ἡ Μοῦσα πόλεως ἐγκρατὴς γενήσεται.—Plato, *Republic*, vi. 12.

"If, then, persons of first-rate philosophical attainments either in the countless ages that are past have been, or in some foreign clime far beyond the times of our horizon at the present moment are, or hereafter shall be constrained by some fate to take the charge of a state, I am prepared to argue to the death in defence of this assertion, that the state described has existed, does exist, yea and will exist wherever the Muse aforesaid has become its mistress. Its realization is no impossibility nor are our speculations impracticable."

IN the autumn of 325 B.C., Alexander the Great and the bulk of his army started to retrace their steps from the East. The great invasion had affected India very little. Persia the Greeks had made their own; India they had barely touched. It is a significant fact that the name of Alexander never occurs in Indian literature before the Mahommedan period. To one man, however, the lesson conveyed by the invasion was plain enough. A certain Chandragupta (the name was corrupted into Sandracottus by the Greeks) saw how easily the disunited Indian States had been subdued by the Macedonians, and he determined to attempt a similar feat himself. An illegitimate son of one of the princes of Magadha, the premier state in Eastern India, Chandragupta was an unscrupulous adventurer. He soon found an opportunity for putting his schemes into effect. Less than two years after Alexander's departure came the news of his death at Babylon, and in the panic which ensued among the Macedonian garrisons of the Panjab, Chandragupta headed a national rising which placed the greater part of North-Western India in his hands. He then turned his attention to his kinsman, the unpopular monarch of Magadha, whom he dethroned, and eventually made himself master of the whole of the Aryavarta, the land between the Himalayas and the Narmada. The results of his masterly policy were seen a few years later, when Seleucus I., King of Syria, tried to repeat Alexander's exploits. Alexander had found it a comparatively easy task to subdue one Indian tribe after another; Seleucus, to his surprise, was confronted with a vast, homogeneous empire, and an army better organized than his own. He was glad to come to terms with his formidable opponent, and to give him in marriage a princess of the Royal House, as a pledge of his friendship. Chandragupta was too far-sighted to care about the scruples of the older Hindu rulers against marriage or intercourse with foreigners. Trade with the West was encouraged; and no doubt the presence of a Greek *râni* at Pataliputra tended to popularize a taste for Western fashions among the aristocracy.

More than one ambassador from Syria resided in India in his reign; and to one of them, Megasthenes, we owe most of our knowledge of the great Indian emperor. He describes him as living among scenes of barbaric opulence; for, like Alexander himself, he had adopted the elaborate ceremonial of the Persian court. A hard, cruel man, he went in constant danger of assassination; he was forced to live in strict seclusion, surrounded by his Amazonian guard of gigantic Greek women, who cut down any one venturing to approach too near.[1] His rule was strict and harsh; mutilation, torture, and capital punishment were inflicted, contrary to Hindu custom. In order to meet the problem of governing an empire far vaster than had ever been known in India before, an elaborate Civil Service was organized, which does credit to the political genius of its founder. The country was divided into provinces, each with its Viceroy reigning at the provincial capital; the administration of the districts was conducted on the ancient Indian system of the *Panchayat*, or Board of Five. In each district there were six of these boards: one superintended the collection of taxes; another assisted them by keeping registers of the population,—births, deaths, and other statistics. Others, again, regulated the manufactures, trade-guilds, and markets. Honesty on the part of the merchants was enforced by the severest penalties, for Indians were justly proud of their reputation for probity in the ancient world.[2] Artisans were under

[1] These were the origin of the "guard of Yavanis," who are a stock feature of the Indian Drama.

[2] Megasthenes says that in the vast camp of Sandracottus the thefts were less than 200 drachmæ (£3) per diem.

the special protection of Government, for the Maurya Emperors were great patrons of art. The enlightened foreign policy of Chandragupta was responsible for the formation of a special board for the purpose of providing for the wants of foreign travellers and merchants. Under the Viceroys were Commissioners and lower officials who superintended the working of the various boards; in addition to them, independent supervisors reported directly to the King upon the administration of the provinces.

This, then, was the vast heritage to which Asoka, grandson of Chandragupta, succeeded in 272 B.C. His father Bindusara had died after an uneventful reign of a quarter of a century. For eleven years he ruled as his predecessors had done, and then an event happened which changed the whole tenor of his life. The kingdom of Kalinga, which lay between the mouths of the Godaveri and Mahanadi rivers, and roughly corresponded to the modern Vizagapatam and Ganjam districts, had became involved in a dispute with its overlord. The usual war of extermination followed. Upwards of one hundred and fifty thousand captives had been made, a hundred thousand had been slain, and countless others had perished miserably of starvation. Neither age nor sex had been spared; even Brahmins and ascetics had perished with the rest. Asoka was filled with remorse at the sight of so much suffering. As a young man, he must have been familiar with the doctrines of Buddhism, for Magadha had been the centre of Gautama's religious activities. In his sorrow, Asoka sought consolation in the teachings of the half-forgotten creed of his boyhood. He called

CAPITAL OF AN ASOKA PILLAR.
Sarnath.
(Photo by the Archæological Survey of India.)

[*To face page* 27.

to his court the famous doctor Upagupta, and bade him expound to him the tenets of his religion. The effect was magical; Asoka was converted to Buddhism, took minor orders in the Church, and set himself, with all the ardour of the convert, to remodel his kingdom upon the precepts of the Dharma. In no country in the world, perhaps, except India, could such an experiment have had any chance of success. The peculiar temperament of the people, together with the admirable administrative system which Asoka had inherited from his grandfather, alone enabled him to carry into effect his Utopian dreams. Fortunately, the details of this great experiment have not been lost in the oblivion which has swallowed up so much of the early history of India; the Emperor's injunctions, regulations, and homilies were recorded in edicts which were issued from time to time and were inscribed upon rocks, or pillars erected for the purpose, in various parts of the country. The lofty moral tone of these edicts indicates clearly enough that India, in the third century B.C., was a highly civilized country; it must, indeed, have compared favourably with the rest of the world of the time, for Greece was sinking fast into a state of corrupt decadence, and Rome, in the throes of her struggle with Carthage, had scarcely yet emerged from barbarism. Education, too, must have been more widely diffused than in later ages; for the presence of these inscriptions, written in the vernacular, proves that reading was a common accomplishment. This was probably due to the Buddhist monks, who have always been enthusiastic in the cause of learning. Burma at the present day is a happy instance of this.

The first result of Asoka's conversion was the determination to abandon warlike undertakings. In future his conquests were to be religious ones. The only invasions he would now countenance were to be carried out by the yellow-robed ascetics, bound upon the peaceful errand of converting the world. These Asoka sent far and wide. Nothing is known of the fate of those whom he despatched to his neighbours the Kings of Greece, Syria, Alexandria, and Epirus; but one mission, at least, had a great and lasting success. The island of Ceylon embraced the Buddhist creed, and the King's own brother, Mahendra, was sent to plant at Anuradhapura a slip of the sacred Bodhi Tree at Gaya, where it may be still seen. But we will let Asoka tell the story in his own words. "In his Majesty's eyes, the chief conquest is that of the Law. For the conquest thus made is full of pleasure. Yet the pleasure produced thereby is a small thing: for His Majesty regards as fruitful only that which concerns the other world. And His Majesty has issued this edict in order that his sons and grandsons may not regard it as their duty to undertake new wars of aggression. If, perchance, they should become involved in war, they should take pleasure in the exercise of patience and gentleness towards their foes, always remembering that the only true conquest is that of Religion. For that alone avails in this world and the next. Let all joy be in effort, for that alone brings happiness in this world and the next."

The practical application of the principles of Buddhism to the everyday affairs of the kingdom led to the abolition of numerous practices, involving unnecessary suffering to men and beasts. The slaughter of animals to stock the royal larders was greatly reduced, and finally abolished altogether. "Formerly, in the kitchens of His Majesty, many hundred thousands of animals were slain for food. Now this has been reduced to three, namely, two peacocks and one antelope, and the antelope not invariably. Even these three are not to be slaughtered in future." Feasts at which animals were sacrificed were forbidden; and various harmless creatures, such as monkeys, squirrels, deer, and various kinds of birds, were protected by special ordinance. Branding, mutilation, even fishing, were declared to be unlawful on certain days, in order that all Nature might have fixed periods of immunity from persecution, and the sacred festivals might not be stained with cruel actions. "She-goats, ewes, and sows, either with young or in milk, and their offspring up to six months, are exempt from slaughter. Forests are not to be burnt, either in mischief or to destroy life. The living must not be fed with the living." Asoka was unable, apparently, to abolish entirely the severe criminal code of his grandfather, but he modified it in several respects. Capital punishment was still enforced, but the criminal was granted three days' respite, during which he received earnest spiritual instruction and consolation. On the anniversary of the King's coronation, there was a general remission of sentences and release of prisoners. One humanitarian reform of the King's is particularly striking, anticipating, as it does, modern ideas by so many centuries: "Everywhere in his domains His Majesty has established hospitals of two kinds, namely, for men and for animals.[1] Medicinal herbs also, for men and for animals, wherever lacking, have been imported and planted. Roots also, and fruits, have been imported. Wells have been dug and trees planted on the high-roads for the refreshment of man and beast." To one class of men Asoka devoted special care, and that was to the aboriginal tribes haunting the forests and mountains on the borders of Aryan India. These poor savages had been looked upon as something less than animals by the caste-bound Hindus, and no doubt were treated with cruelty and disdain. But in the royal eyes all men were brothers, and the King especially enjoins the gentle treatment of these outcastes. Even when found guilty, as doubtless they often were, of robbing or pillaging, the effects of persuasion and religious teaching were to be tried. "Even upon the jungle-folk in his domain His Majesty looks kindly and seeks their conversion. They are exhorted to give up their evil ways in order to escape punishment. His Majesty desires that all animate beings should enjoy security, peace of mind, joyfulness." "If you ask," he tells his officials, "What is the King's command with regard to the unconquered tribes on the border, or what does he desire the borderers to understand, the answer is, that the King desires that they should not be afraid of him, that they should trust him, and should receive from his hand happiness and not sorrow. They should grasp the fact that the King will bear patiently with them, and that for his

[1] The Jains have similar respect for life. In Bombay the visitor may see an animal hospital kept up by them—the Pinjrapole. Hospitals were founded in Ceylon by King Duthu Gamani (161 B.C.).

sake they should follow the Law, and so profit in this world and the next. Now is it for you to do your part, and to make the people trust me, and realize that *the King is even as a father unto us. He loves us as himself. We are to him as his own children.*"

The King's conception of his own duties is a high one, and he expects a correspondingly lofty standard on the part of his subordinates. As the true Father of the People he is ready at any hour of the day or night to receive petitions or to hear complaints.[1] "Whether I am dining, or in the harem, or in bed, or driving, or in the garden, the reporters are to report to me upon the business of the people. And if by any chance I give a verbal order to any official, and if in carrying it out a dispute arises or fraud is committed, I have commanded the whole matter to be reported to me at any hour or place, for I am never fully satisfied with my efforts. I must work for the common weal; and the way to achieve this is by effort and despatch. For this end I toil—to discharge my debt to living beings, and to make a few happy in this world and the next." "His Majesty does not believe that glory or renown brings much profit, unless in both the present and the future my people obediently hearken to the Law and keep its behests. In this way only His Majesty seeks for renown. Whatsoever exertions His Majesty makes, they are all for the sake of the life to come, in order that every one may be free from the peril of vice."

[1] This is an essential feature of the ideal Indian King. A pretty legend relates that Elala, a Tamil king of Ceylon, had a bell hung over his bed; the bell-rope hung outside, and any one who had a grievance might pull it at any hour of the day or night. The same story is told of the Emperor Jehangir.

Asoka was exacting in the demands which he made on his civil officers. Like the King, they were to regard themselves as the fathers of the people, and work for no other end: "My Commissioners are set over many thousands of my subjects. I have granted them a free hand in the award of punishments and rewards, in order that they may perform their duties in a fearless spirit, and that the nation may benefit thereby. They will ascertain the causes of happiness and discontent, and will see that the officials in charge of religious duties exhort the people to piety, that they may profit in this life thereafter. My Commissioners zealously fulfil my orders; my Overseers will exhort them, when necessary, to further efforts in order to win my favour. Just as a man who has entrusted his child to a skilled nurse feels secure, saying to himself, 'This skilled nurse is zealous for the care of my child's happiness'; even so, my Commissioners have been appointed for the purpose of ensuring the welfare of the nation. And in order that they may perform their duties fearlessly, securely, and quietly, they have been given a free hand in the matter of punishments and awards." "Whatever my views are, I desire them to be carried out by certain means. Now, in my opinion the best means to do this is by carrying out my instructions. You have been set over many thousands of human beings that you may win the love of good men. All men are my children. Just as I desire prosperity and happiness, now and hereafter, for my children, I desire it for all men. You do not all appear fully to have grasped this truth. Individuals here and there have endeavoured to carry it out, but not all.

Take heed, then, for the principle is a sound one. Sometimes, for instance, a man is punished or imprisoned unjustly, and when this happens many others are rendered discontented. In that case you must find out what is right. With certain dispositions success is impossible, to wit, in the case of envious, lazy, harsh, impatient, indolent persons. Pray that you be not one of these. The secret of the whole matter is perseverance and patience. The indolent man is unable to rouse himself to act; but one should be always pressing forward. . . . For this purpose, in accordance with the Law, I shall send forth on circuit every five years such officers as are of a merciful disposition and are mindful of the sanctity of life, who know my purpose, and who are likely to carry it out."[1] This important edict was primarily addressed to the officials in the newly conquered province of Kalinga; it was, however, of universal application, and copies were doubtless erected in various provinces. These regulations were not only to be set up in conspicuous places, but to be read at certain seasons in public, "even if there were only a single person to listen"; by this means it was assured that no one could suffer from petty tyranny on the part of the officials without knowing that a complaint addressed to the Viceroy, the Overseers, or to the Emperor himself, would obtain a ready hearing.

The majority of the edicts, however, were published for the purpose of inculcating religion among

[1] This admirable sermon on the duties of civil officers is as true to-day as it was in the third century B.C.; so little has India changed.

the people. Asoka's religion is of an intensely practical kind. It is mainly ethical, insisting upon reverence towards parents and religious teachers, purity, honesty, and mercy to man and beast. Of philosophic doctrines no mention is made; nothing, for instance, is said of Nirvana, or the ultimate release of the soul, of rebirth or retribution. Men are merely told that the consequence of good actions will be happiness "in this world and the next." The ordinary Buddhist, or Hindu for the matter of fact, looks no further than rebirth in the Heaven of his favourite deity, and Asoka wisely confines himself to this. Virtue, in his opinion, brings its own reward. One of the earliest edicts inculcates the traditional reverence for parents and teachers, which is such a beautiful feature of Indian life. "Honour thy father and thy mother: establish firmly the law of mercy to all living creatures: speak the truth. These are the virtues which must be practised. The pupil must respect his teachers: courtesy towards kinsmen must be observed. This is the nature of piety from the times of yore: this leads to length of days, and this is how men must act." "Thus says His Majesty: the Law is an excellent thing. But in what does the Law consist? In abstinence from wickedness, in doing good, in compassion, liberality, patience and purity in life." "Man recognizes his good actions. 'This and this good action I have done,' he says. But he fails to recognize his evil actions: he never says, 'This and this evil action I have done.' Self-examination is indeed difficult: yet a man should guard against the sins of cruelty, anger, pride, and jealousy, knowing that these lead to sin. Remember that the one course may be profitable for this world; but the other profits also for the next." "There is no charity so meritorious as the charity of religion—religious friendship, propagation of religion, kinship in religion. In this does it consist: in kindness to menials and dependants, obedience to parents, liberality to friends, kinsfolk, and holy men, and mercy to all living creatures." Lastly, Asoka insists on the grand principle of religious toleration. Himself a Buddhist, he realizes that all creeds alike have the same great aims in view, and are entitled to equal consideration. The attitude of this ancient King contrasts strangely with the narrow sectarian views of many preachers of religion to-day. Asoka's missionaries were imbued with a higher spirit. "His Majesty does reverence to men of all religions, whether laymen or ascetics, by gifts and various forms of reverence. His Majesty, however, cares less for gifts or outward forms of respect than for the growth of the essential doctrines of religion. These doctrines assume different forms in different creeds, but the essence of them all is restraint of speech, namely, that no one should exalt his own creed or disparage that of his neighbour unreasonably. Disparagement should be allowed only for sufficient reasons: all religions command our respect for one reason or another. By acting in this manner, a man not only does a service to the creeds of his neighbours, but he also wins respect for his own creed; while abusing his neighbours' beliefs, he does harm to his own. The man who praises his own particular form of religion and sneers at that of others, merely in order to enhance his own, in reality inflicts upon it the most grievous injury. Harmony in religion, then, should be our aim, and willingness to hearken to the forms of religious belief of others. His Majesty hopes that all sects will hear much religious instruction and hold sound beliefs. The members of all creeds are to be informed that His Majesty cares less for gifts or outward forms of respect than for the growth of the essentials of religion and the spirit of toleration."

Asoka reigned for forty years at Pataliputra. Of the events of his long career, except the conquest of Kalinga, the conversion of Ceylon, and the publication of the edicts, we know little or nothing; for no reliance can be placed in the grotesque monkish legends which afterwards collected round the name of the greatest of the Buddhist emperors. We may say, as Gibbon said of a famous Roman monarch, that "His reign is marked by the rare advantage of furnishing very few materials for history, which is indeed little more than the register of the crimes, the follies, and misfortune of mankind." After his conversion he became a lay disciple; four years later he took full orders. He was a great builder. His grandfather had made special arrangements for the protection and encouragement of the hereditary crafts-guilds; Asoka taught them to work in stone. Hence his monuments are the earliest examples of Indian art which have survived the progress of time. The great tope at Sanchi, the noble lion-pillars at Sarnath and Lauriya-Nandangarh, and the exquisitely-polished caves at Baraber near Gaya, are all that remain now of his extensive buildings. Centuries after his death a Chinese pilgrim gazed upon the ruins of the Imperial palace with awe, declaring that the gigantic stones with their elaborate carving were "the work of no mortal hands." There is no reason to consider Asoka an isolated phenomenon in early Indian history: the rare glimpses afforded to us of Vikramaditya, Harsha, and others, when the veil of deep obscurity which rests on pre-Mohammedan India is for a moment lifted, reveal to us a well-governed, prosperous land, with an enlightened administration, and a highly civilized population. Asoka's edicts would have been thrown away upon an ignorant, brutal, or vicious nation. They confirm the statements made by such independent witnesses as Megasthenes in the third century B.C., and Hiuen Tsiang in the seventh century A.D., that in ancient India the standard of morality was extraordinarily high.

One is tempted to compare Asoka with Akbar. Both realized that government, to succeed in India, must be of a personal nature, and based upon religious principles. "The success of the government and the fulfilment of the needs of the subject," writes Akbar's biographer, "Depend upon the manner in which the King spends his time." The words might be Asoka's own. Nowhere is Carlyle's doctrine of hero-worship so well illustrated as in the history of India; for it is the history, not of institutions but of men,—the leaders, religious and secular (and the line between the hero as priest and king is only faintly drawn), of the nation from age to age.

III

THE INDO-GREEK DYNASTIES OF THE PANJAB.

III

THE INDO-GREEK DYNASTIES OF THE PANJAB.

Bâkhdhîm s'rîrãm eredhvô drafshãm. "Bactra the beautiful, crowned with banners."—*Vendidad*, i. 7.

FAR away in the rolling steppes of Turkestan, many days' journey from the frontier passes of India, lies the ancient city of Balkh, the Bactra of the Greeks and Bakhdhi of the ancient Persians. Bactra is one of those places—like Byzantium, for instance, and Alexandria—which is marked out by its geographical position to play a great part in the world's history. It is a meeting-place of nations. The three great trade routes of Asia, from India, from China, and from the coasts of the Black Sea and the Levant, converged here, and in the bazaars of Balkh, from time immemorial, Greek, Indian, Chinese, and the Turki nomad of the steppes, have met and bartered their wares. Its strategic importance, too, was very great. An army occupying Balkh menaced China and India alike, and could levy toll on the land-borne trade of half the continent of Asia. Besides this, Balkh was the great frontier fortress of the Aryan world, and on its integrity depended the safety of not only Persia, but India, from the incursions of the hordes of Central Asia. Long before the coming of the Aryans, Balkh must have been occupied by the Scythian tribes, who worshipped there, in a shrine of immemorial antiquity, the goddess Anahid, with her cloak of otter skins and her starry halo.[1] Then, about two thousand years before Christ, came the Aryan invasion, sweeping on westward into Media and Persia, and southward, over the mountains, into Hindustan. A small body of Iranians, as the northern Aryans came to be called, attracted, no doubt, by the fertile Bactrian oasis, elected to settle in the country, where they dwelt, cut off from their kinsmen in the south by the mountains, and from those in the west by the great Carmanian Desert. Outnumbered by the aboriginal populace, the Iranian knights built themselves forts on the abrupt mountain peaks which are a feature of the country, and thence ruled their subjects in safety. Years went on, and the Iranian peoples of Western Asia came to look upon the ancient city of Balkh, with its stern walls and its venerable shrine, as one of the most sacred cities in their land. It was certainly one of the earliest habitations of the Aryan tribes of which we have any knowledge. Hither, too, came the prophet Zarathustra with his kindred, about the time when Gautama Buddha was preaching his earliest sermons in far distant Benares (in the reign, it is said, of the King Gustaspa), and attained great power in the court of the Bactrian monarch. It is even recorded in the old legends that he died there, slain, during a Scythian rising, with all his folk, by the altar of the sacred fire.

[1] Avesta Hymns in the *Sacred Books of the East*, ii. p. 79.

We hear little more of the city of Bactra until Darius the Great annexed Eastern Iran to the Persian Empire, and made it the base for the great invasion of the Panjab which started along the ancient road from Balkh to the Khyber Pass, and ended by annexing the rich valley of the Indus, with its trade in fine linen, spices, jewels, and gold dust. It was from the Persians that the Indian tribes of the North-West Frontier acquired the ancient Kharoshthi script, an Aramaic alphabet running from right to left, which remained in use among them for many centuries afterwards. Again silence broods over Bactria for many years; we hear dim rumours of Bactrian troops being employed by the Great King in his long wars with the Greeks, and we know that the satrap of Bactria, always, by virtue of his position, a Prince of the Blood, became more and more independent as the Persian Empire began to break up. The climax came when Alexander, in 331 B.C., beat the Persians in the great battle of Gaugamela. Darius fled, accompanied by his cousin Bessus, Governor of Bactria, hoping to make a last stand among the mountain fastnesses of his eastern domains. On the way, however, he was murdered by his treacherous kinsman, who was determined that he, if any, should restore the fallen fortunes of Iran. But Alexander was no ordinary leader. At first he hurried at the heels of Bessus along the great caravan route which skirts the southern shores of the Caspian Sea, but hearing of rebellions among the confederates of Bessus in Aria and Drangiana, he suddenly turned southwards, surprised Herat, and made his way along the Helmand valley, determined to enter Bactria from the south. We need not follow in detail the horrors of the march over the Hindu Kush—an enterprise which alone puts Alexander on a level with Hannibal and Napoleon—or of the final advance upon Bactria. In 328 B.C., the weary but elated Macedonians stood within the frowning ramparts of the famous city, the furthest outpost of the Aryan world. They gazed about them with amazement, noting the huge battlements, the splendid temple, rich with the gifts of the Persian monarchs, and the spacious suburbs. They were shocked, however, at the barbarous Scythian habit of giving the bodies of the dead to dogs to devour. The streets, they said, were littered with bones, and Alexander suppressed the practice. Alexander, however, had not reached the limit of his ambitions in the reduction of the province of Bactria. Before him lay the rich plains of India, and thither, after founding a huge military colony in the conquered province in 327, he set out. Of his adventures in India we need not here speak at length. He defeated the greatest of the princes of the Panjab in a pitched battle, but thwarted by a rebellion of his weary soldiers, was unable to carry out his scheme of invading the Gangetic plain, which would have anticipated by centuries the achievements of the Moghuls. Alexander then turned to other ideas. Marching down the Indus, in spite of desperate resistance from the various tribes which barred his way, he determined to carry into effect the plans of his great predecessor, Darius of Persia. All along the Indus sprang up colonies, factories, and trading emporia, with wharves for cargo-boats and a port at the mouth of the river. Alexander's idea, no doubt, was to establish a regular trade between the rich Indus valley and the mouth of the Euphrates. The project, like all that proceeded from the brain of the great Macedonian, was fraught with immense and far-reaching possibilities. While Nearchus was feeling his way up the Persian Gulf, Alexander, with the bulk of the Macedonian army, tried to find a land route through the Mekran desert. The result of the latter experiment was disastrous, but the main objects of the expedition were successfully achieved. Modern readers smile at the accounts of these old Greek seamen, with the frights they sustained from the tidal bore of the Indus, and the schools of whales "blowing" in the waters of the Indian Ocean; but the world owes almost as much to these intrepid navigators as to their later successors, Columbus and Vasco de Gama.

All was well in the vast empire, when suddenly the news spread from port to port that Alexander had died at Babylon of malarial fever (323 B.C.). Every one was panic-stricken. Rebellions sprang up in every province. The troops in Bactria started marching back to the west, while in the Indus valley, Eudamus, commander-in-chief of the Indian Alexandria, collected all the plunder he could lay hands on, and made his way across the Khyber Pass with all speed. With him went the majority of the Greeks, though a considerable body of them, probably men who had become naturalized and had married native wives, remained behind in the country. The political power of Greece in the Panjab, however, was quite at an end, chiefly owing to the schemes of that great adventurer and leader Chandragupta Maurya

(317 B.C.). For the next ten years India was free from Greek invasion, and under the stern rule of Chandragupta she prospered exceedingly. "He had freed the country from external rule," says Justin, "but he reduced it to slavery to himself." Traces of his organization of the land may be gathered from the fragments of Megasthenes, and from the references in the edicts of his grandson Asoka. Hence it is not surprising that when Seleucus, in 305 B.C., after annexing Bactria to the Syrian Empire, tried to repeat the exploits of Alexander, he found himself grievously disappointed. Instead of attacking and defeating the local rajas in detail, he found himself face to face with a compact force of some 600,000 troops! The chagrined monarch retreated in confusion without risking an engagement.

We must now turn our attention once more to the principality of Bactria. For fifty years it remained an outlying province of Syria, enjoying a large measure of autonomy, and profiting greatly by the increase of trade between India and the west which resulted from the pro-Hellenic tendencies of the Maurya dynasty. But about 250 B.C., Diodotus, the Bactrian satrap, determined to strike for freedom, in imitation of a similar movement on the part of the neighbouring nation of Parthia. The Seleucid monarch, busy with Egypt and dissensions nearer home, was compelled to look helplessly on; and when his successor, Antiochus the Great, in 209 B.C., tried to subdue the rebels, he found the walls of Bactria too strong to storm, and after a long and desperate siege he acknowledged the independence of the province and withdrew. Syria, menaced by the growing powers of Rome in the west and Parthia in the north, could ill afford to destroy the chief bulwark of her land against Scythian invasions from beyond the Oxus.

It would have been well, indeed, had the Bactrian monarchs confined themselves to this *rôle;* but the fatal temptation offered by the rich lands of the Panjab was too strong for them. There seems to be an irresistible impulse always driving the inhabitants of Central Asia southwards; and the poor quality of the great part of the Bactrian territory made expansion a physical necessity. Besides, advance to the east was rendered impossible by the Parthians, the hated rivals of Bactria, ever ready to harass and attack their neighbours. Lastly, the break-up of the Maurya dynasty had thrown India into the state of periodical anarchy which has always invited the attention of invaders. Of the great achievements of Demetrius, son of Euthydemus, the hero of the great siege, we know unfortunately very little. But our information is sufficient to show that his chief motive was to benefit the trade of his country by securing the trade routes to China and the Arabian Sea. The mountain passes of Sarikol, the coasts of Kathiawar and Kach, together with the fertile Indus valley, fell once more into Greek hands, and a mighty capital, called by the conqueror Euthydemia, after his father, rose on the site of the ancient city of Sâgala.[1] Sâgala was destined to be the centre of Indo-Greek power till the final extinction of the

[1] It has been identified with Sialkot, Shorkot, and Chuniot by different authorities; but no really satisfactory conclusion as to its site has been arrived at.

dynasty about a century and a half later. The wonderful Bactrian coins which have come down to us (almost the only memorials we possess of this far-off remnant of Greek civilization) depict Euthydemus as a strong, masterful man, wearing a helmet in the shape of an elephant's head, in token, perhaps, of the conquest of India. Unfortunately Euthydemus did not end his days in peace; his long absence in India encouraged a rebellion on the part of Eucratides, who finally deposed him, only to be murdered in his turn by his son, who declared that his father was a public enemy, and cast his body to the dogs. Unfortunately, we do not know the cause of this indictment, but the retribution which always falls upon a nation torn by internal strife was not long in overtaking the kingdom of Bactria. For years they had neglected the *rôle* of protecting the country south of the Oxus from the Scythian hordes; the great garrison town of Furthest Alexandria, which ever since the days of Cyrus the Great had watched over the fords of the Jaxartes, had doubtless been denuded of troops for the Indian wars of Euthydemus, and now the barbarians, sweeping down through Sogdiana into Bactria, forced the Greeks to evacuate their capital *en masse*, and to retire to their new kingdom of Sâgala beyond the Khyber. Drained, as Justin says, of their life-blood by constant fighting, they found resistance to the invading tribes impossible; while the Parthians, who had not wasted their strength on ambitious projects, resisted the new-comers with complete success. And so the Greeks settled down to their kingdom in the Panjab, to enact the last phase in the gallant but fruitless drama of the invasion of Alexander. For the story of many of the succeeding monarchs, we are indebted largely to the coins. These shew for some years the brilliant workmanship of the Bactrian coiners, and the names of the kings—Pantaleon, Agathocles, Strato, Amyntas—and the like—remain purely Greek. But the subjects of the kingdom of Sâgala became slowly but surely absorbed in the native population. They also took up largely the religion of their neighbours, Buddhism and Hinduism. Traces of this are to be seen in the inscriptions and emblems appearing on the coins, where we find on the obverse the Greek inscription and type, and on the reverse the figure of a dancing-girl, or a Buddhist *Stûpa* with a Prakrit motto.

Of only one of the Indo-Greek princes can we relate anything which may be termed definitely personal. This is the great Menander, whose fame has survived in the Buddhist dialogues, the *Questions of Milinda*, and of whom we have just so much information as to make us wish we knew more of the mighty king who was probably the last independent Greek monarch in history.

Menander was born, possibly about 180 B.C., on an island of the Indus, named Kalasi, not far from the great town of Alexandria-on-Indus, at the junction of the Five Rivers. Some twenty years later he succeeded to the throne of Sâgala. Early in his reign he undertook the reconquest of the Indus valley with its trade routes and ports, imitating the exploits of his ancestor Demetrius, with whom he is constantly compared by the geographers. In the Buddhist treatise referred to above, we hear much of the glories of the capital of the Yavana monarch. Within its streets met men of every nation—the merchants of Benares with their filmy muslins, the Greek and Arab seamen of Alexandria and the Red Sea ports who had come up from Broach or Pattala, the Seres from beyond the Great Wall with silk, jewellers and vendors of those strange spices and unguents, malobathrum, spikenard, cassia, pepper and the like, which were consumed in ever-increasing quantities with the growth of luxury in the cities of the West. Even Pataliputra itself could hardly vie with the magnificence of the Greek capital, with its parks and open spaces, and its broad streets and stately marble mansions rising to the sky, in the language of Eastern hyperbole, "like the peaks of the snowy Himalayas." It was probably about this time that Menander became a convert to the creed of Gautama. It is a strange picture—the conversion of the great monarch of the West, the last heir to the conquests of Alexander, to a creed so impregnated with the mystic spirit of the East. With a vivid touch, the author of the *Questions* describes how the sage Nâgasena with his monks wended his way into the palace of the king, and how their yellow robes gleamed among the marble pillars, "lighting up the palace like lamps, and bringing into it a breath of the divine breezes from the heights where the saints have their dwelling-place."

Perhaps it was in the cause of his new faith that Menander undertook the expedition against the kingdom of Magadha, of which we hear faint echoes in many scattered passages of Hindu literature. After the break-up of the Maurya dynasty, the usurper Pushpamitra Sunga had seized the throne, and had deserted the enlightened creed of Asoka for the ancient religion of the Brahmins. Menander's chief object was to imitate Asoka in bringing all Northern India under the sway of the Buddha. The war began with a conflict on the western borders of the Sunga monarch's domains. Chitor and Oude successively fell, and a curious story, related in the drama entitled the *Malavikagnimitra*, tells how a party of Greek horsemen all but captured the sacred horse released by Pushpamitra to wander for the appointed time before being offered in solemn sacrifice. The Horse Sacrifice was a solemn rite celebrated by a successful monarch to mark the completion of his conquests. The victim, accompanied by a guard, wanders for a year in the conquered territory, challenging any one, who desires to dispute its owner's supremacy, to capture it. On this occasion the guard consisted of Vasumitra, the king's grandson, and a hundred Rajput knights. It was only with difficulty that they beat off the sudden charge of the Yavana troopers on the banks of the Sindhu river.

Even the Hindu writers, indifferent as they usually are to historical events, note with dismay the advance of the Western army. "The Yavanas were besieging Saketa and Madhyamikâ," is an example of the imperfect tense given by the contemporary grammarian Patanjali. "When the viciously valiant Yavanas," says the author of the *Gargi Samhita*, "after reducing Saketa, the Panchala country and Mathura, reach the royal capital of Pataliputra, the land will fall into chaos." Menander even reached the banks of the Son, the river on which Patna stands, surpassing thereby the achievements of Alexander himself, says

Strabo. But further he was not destined to go. "The fiercely fighting Yavanas," we are told, "did not tarry long in the Middle Land; a terrible war had broken out in their own land." What that war was we cannot tell: it may have been a Saka or Parthian invasion, or a rebellion among the Greek princes of the Panjab. Whatever it was, Menander, baulked of his great schemes, had to return. One brief glimpse of him we get, this time from Plutarch, before the curtain rings down upon the scene. According to a Siamese tradition, Menander, following the example of his great prototype Asoka, took the yellow robe and attained the rank of an *arhat;* and death found the warrior saint, says Plutarch, still fighting against his numerous foes. As in the case of Gautama Buddha himself, a great contest arose over his ashes, but finally they were divided among the representatives of the several states, and each taking his portion, erected over it a gigantic *dâgaba* in his own country. "In all the land of India," says the author of the *Questions,* "there was no such monarch as Milinda Raja. He acquired great riches, and his army was powerful and well-trained."

After the death of Menander, Indo-Greek power in the Panjab collapsed rapidly. A host of petty princes arose, known to us only by their coins. These were gradually superseded by native rajas, who often restrike the coins of their predecessors; and finally a new enemy, in the shape of the great nomad tribe of the Yueh-chi, appeared from beyond the Khyber. The Yueh-chi had ousted the Sakas from Bactria, and after overrunning that land, a clan known as the Kushans found their way into India. The story is eloquently but silently related by the coins. The last Greek prince, Hermæus, strikes first coins in his own name, and then in conjunction with the Kushan raja Kadphises. Finally Hermæus disappears, and Kadphises reigns alone. Thus ended Indo-Greek rule in the Panjab. It was the last attempt of a European race to govern India until the fatal day, fourteen hundred years later, when the thunder of Portuguese guns was heard beyond the bar by the astonished citizens of Calicut. The Greeks had exerted singularly little influence upon India. Alexander, so celebrated in Persian literature, is unnoticed in India books, and Menander was chiefly celebrated because of his conversion to Buddhism. A single pillar, the work of an Indo-Greek artist, himself a votary of Krishna, has been unearthed in Western India, and a few Greeks appear among the pious donors to the Karla Caves and other Buddhist shrines. The Greek invasions of India had left the country unaffected.

> "The East bowed down before the blast
> In silent, deep disdain:
> She let the legions thunder past,
> And plunged in thought again."

IV

CHINESE PILGRIMS IN INDIA.

IV

CHINESE PILGRIMS IN INDIA.

FA HIAN, *c.* 400 A.D.
HIUEN TSIANG, 629–645 A.D.

Buddhism has always been a proselytizing religion. Gautama himself had sent his disciples far and wide to spread the Dhamma, and the great Emperor Asoka had visions of converting, not only India, but the whole of the known world, to the creed which he had embraced so enthusiastically. History is silent as to the fate of the missionaries whom he sent to the courts of Antiochus and Ptolemy, and to the distant monarchs of Macedonia, Cyrene, and Epirus; but Ceylon still bears witness to the success of his activity nearer home. It was reserved, however, for another age to see the spread of Buddhism to the vast Mongolian nations north of the Himalayas, where it still numbers millions of converts, though long since dead in the land where Gautama lived and laboured. About 165 B.C., a Scythian tribe had been forced by pressure from behind to cross the Jaxartes, and descend upon the fertile plains of Bactria (the territory adjacent to the modern Balkh). Balkh at that time was in the hands of a powerful Greek dynasty, the descendants of military colonists settled there by

Alexander. The hordes, however, managed to push them gradually southward, till they took refuge in the Panjab, where once again they contrived to build up a considerable kingdom. Under their great King Menander they became for a time the foremost power in India, and very largely embraced the Buddhist creed; for Buddhism made a special appeal to the casteless adventurers who from time to time swooped down upon those fertile plains. Finally, however, the Indo-Greeks became disorganized, and again fell an easy prey to their former conquerors, who had followed them across the Hindu Kush. The Yueh-chi, or rather the Kushan clan of that great tribe, rapidly rose to power. The Kushan Empire reached its highest point under Kanishka, in the first century after Christ, who ruled over the whole of India north of the Narmada, together with the greater part of Tibet, Afghanistan and Turkestan. Kanishka became an enthusiastic convert to Buddhism, and it appears probable that the teachings of the Master reached China in his reign. When Kanishka conquered Khotan—Eastern Turkestan—he took certain Chinese hostages back to India, one of them being a son of the Emperor. During their long exile in the Panjab, these hostages were hospitably entertained at various monasteries, and doubtless they learned from the monks something of their religion. In any case, the conquest of the provinces on the Chinese frontier brought Buddhism to the very borders of the country. Monasteries sprang up in Tibet and Khotan, and from them, as well as from the caravans which began to go to and fro between India and China, rumours of the new creed must have spread northwards. China

PRAJNÂPÂRÁMITÂ.

A Mahayana Goddess from Java.

(By permission of Dr. A. K. Coomaraswamy.)

[*To face page* 59.

was ripe for conversion. In spite of their earnest disposition, the Chinese had not succeeded in evolving a religion of their own. A vague system of ancestor worship, and a series of rather dreary discourses upon ethical subjects, were all that their own teachers had produced. Confucius, an early contemporary of Gautama, is supposed to have prophesied that a Sage should arise in the West. The fame of Buddha may possibly have reached his ears.[1] However this may be, Buddhism began to attract ever-increasing attention in China during the first three centuries of the Christian era. Certain difficulties, however, stood in the way: the journey from China to India was long and dangerous; the Indian tongue was difficult to acquire, and Chinese was ill-adapted for rendering abstruse and novel metaphysical terms. Such manuscripts as reached China were often imperfect and ill-understood.

Certain devout Chinamen, however, determined to overcome these obstacles. Inspired by a desire to benefit their fellow-countrymen, these brave scholars set out from time to time to India, in order to visit the scenes of the Master's life on earth, to study the language in which he taught, and to bring back manuscripts of the Sacred Books yet unknown north of the Himalayas. Nothing could exceed the devotion of these old travellers, who spent years in crossing the burning deserts and snowy mountains in fulfilment of their self-imposed tasks. Some perished of cold or thirst; others were killed by brigands; others again were drowned in attempting to return to China

[1] The story is vague and doubtful. Capital of course was made of it by the early Christian missionaries.

by sea. "Never," says Mr. Beal, "Did more devoted pilgrims leave their native country to encounter the perils of travel in foreign and distant lands; never did disciples more ardently desire to gaze on the sacred vestiges of their religion; never did men endure greater sufferings by desert, mountain, and sea, than these simple-minded, earnest Buddhist priests. And that such courage, religious devotion, and power of endurance, should be exhibited by men so sluggish, as we think, as the Chinese, is very surprising, and may perhaps arouse some consideration." The records of their travels, besides being of the greatest intrinsic interest, are of first-rate importance to the student of medieval Indian History. India has no history of her own, and the observations of these ancient visitors supplement in a remarkable way the fragmentary remains in the shape of coins, inscriptions, and legends, which are all that have otherwise come down to us.[1] It is, of course, disappointing to find that the monkish chroniclers have taken pains to record stories about miraculous relics of fabulous power, dragons which devoured travellers, and grotesque legends of medieval saints, to the exclusion of information which would be priceless to the modern historian; but, considered as a whole, the interest and value of their narratives can hardly be over-estimated.

Of the numerous pilgrims who visited India between the fourth and seventh centuries A.D., the most important were Fa Hian and Hiuen Tsiang. Fa

[1] Besides this, the Chinese versions of the Buddhist books are of the utmost value to scholars. Many books of which the originals are now lost have come down to us in Chinese.

Hian is the first pilgrim who has left any record of his adventures: Hiuen Tsiang composed an important itinerary, which is supplemented by a charming biography written by one of his pupils, and he is rightly regarded in China as one of the greatest of Buddhist scholars. It must be remembered that the Buddhism of these travellers was very different from the simple creed taught by Gautama. Gautama denied the existence of the soul, and found no place for prayer or belief in God: later Buddhists, especially those who, like Hiuen Tsiang, belonged to the Mahayanist school, found this austere philosophy quite insufficient for their needs. Gautama, when he passed away from earth, ceased to exist: Buddhists, not unnaturally, found more consolation in worshipping Maitreya, the benignant spirit destined one day to be incarnate as Gautama's earthly successor, who, until that time arrives, dwells in the Tushita heaven, surrounded by the spirits of those happy devotees who have been re-born into his presence as a reward for their devotion to him upon earth. Philosophers like Hiuen Tsiang found no difficulty in reconciling these mystical speculations with the bare system of Gautama, of which they regarded them as the natural development, just as the pious Catholic regards his stately ritual as a legitimate deduction from the teaching of Jesus of Galilee.

Fa Hian set out from his home in China, with five companions, in the year 400 A.D. His main purpose was to obtain correct and full copies of certain treatises upon conduct, which form an important part of Buddhist religious literature. After travelling for about nine months, the pilgrims finally found themselves at Tung Wang, a frontier fortress on the confines of the Lop Nor desert. Assisted by the prefect of the city, the party struck out across the sands to the little kingdom of Cherchen. The journey was a trying one; for seventeen days they toiled across the barren waste, seeing neither beast nor bird, while the path was marked with ominous skeletons and carcases. After resting at Cherchen for a month, they set out along the Tarim river to a country called Wu-ki, on the north-east corner of the Tarim Desert. Here they met with a cold reception, probably on account of doctrinal differences; so, starting once more, they skirted the Muzart mountains for a while, and then, following the Khotan river, arrived, safe but weary, in the hospitable kingdom of Khotan. This was in Fa Hian's days a fertile and flourishing state; now, owing to some mysterious climatic change, the sands have swept down and obliterated the whole country. Explorers have recently unearthed lines of tree-trunks marking the sites of what were once groves, gardens, and orchards, and here and there they have found remnants of the *stupas*, decorated with statues in the Indo-Greek style, at which the pilgrims must have returned thanks for their safe arrival.

Fresh perils, however, awaited them. After a prolonged halt, the party pushed on to Yarkand, and then, following the Yarkand river, slowly and laboriously made their way across the mountains in the direction of India. Fa Hian graphically describes how they crossed a tributary of the Indus by a rope-ladder under extraordinary difficulties. "The road was difficult and broken, with steep crags and precipices in the way. The mountain-side is simply a stone wall standing up ten thousand feet. Looking down, the sight is confused, and on going forward there is no sure foothold. Below is a river called the Sin-tu-ho.[1] In old days men bored through the rocks to make a way, and spread outside ladders, of which there are seven hundred steps to pass in all. Having descended the ladders, we proceed by a hanging rope-bridge and cross the river." Here, in a little Buddhist state which they found nestling in the northern extremity of the Swat valley, they rested awhile, before pushing on to the great frontier city of Peshawar. At Peshawar the party of pilgrims began to break up. Three, disheartened by the long journey, turned back home; another died in a monastery; a third perished in a blizzard between Peshawar and Jellalabad. The scene is pathetically described. "Hiu King was unable to go further. His mouth was covered with white froth; and at last he addressed Fa Hian and said, 'I am beyond recovery; do you leave me and press on lest you all perish.' And so he died: Fa Hian cherished him and called him by his familiar name, but all in vain." And so, with a single companion, the stout pilgrim at last reached the land of his desires. His account of India as he found it presents us with a valuable picture of the Gupta Empire, of which we otherwise know so little. The high-sounding inscription on the pillar at Allahabad affords a tantalizing glimpse into the conquests and literary achievements of the great Samudragupta. His son, Vikramaditya, who must have been reigning when Fa Hian travelled through the land, was equally

[1] The Indus. The scene here described is not uncommon in the wild mountains and precipitous gorges of the Swat country.

famous; a mighty warrior and a successful statesman, he was also a patron of the Arts. At his brilliant court the celebrated Nine Gems of Sanskrit Literature were assembled; and the prince himself is said to have been an accomplished dramatist, poet, and musician. Of the monarch, however, Fa Hian, with a monk's indifference to worldly things, makes no mention. On the other hand, he speaks in glowing terms of the justice, clemency, and efficiency of the government. "The inhabitants," he says, "are prosperous and happy. Only those who farm the royal estates pay any portion of the produce as rent; and they are not bound to remain in possession longer than they like.[1] The King inflicts no corporal punishment, but merely fines the offenders, and even those convicted of incitement to rebellion, after repeated attempts, are only punished with the loss of the right hand. The Chief Ministers have fixed salaries allotted to them. The people of the country drink no intoxicants and kill no animals for food, except the Chandalas or Pariahs; and these alone eat garlic or onions. The Pariahs live outside the walls; if they enter the town, they have to strike a gong with a piece of wood to warn passers-by not to touch them.

"In this country they do not keep swine or fowls, and do not deal in cattle; they have no shambles or wine-shops in their market-places. In commerce they use cowrie-shells.[2] The Pariahs alone hunt and sell flesh. Down from the time of the Lord Buddha's

[1] Compare the similar custom among the Sinhalese, recorded by Knox.

[2] Only for small change, of course. The Gupta monarchs issued a fine and abundant coinage in gold and silver. See p. 80.

Nirvana the kings, chief men, and householders have raised *viharas* for the monks, and have provided for their support by endowing them with fields, houses, gardens, servants, and cattle. These Church-lands are guaranteed to them by copperplate grants, which are handed down from reign to reign, and no one has had the temerity to cancel them. All the resident priests, who are allotted cells in the *viharas*, have beds, mats, food, and drink supplied to them; they pass their time in performing acts of mercy, in reciting the Scriptures, or in meditation. When a stranger arrives at the monastery, the senior priests escort him to the guest-house, carrying his robes and his alms-bowl for him. They offer him water to wash his feet, and oil for anointing, and prepare a special meal for him. After he has rested awhile they ask him his rank in the priesthood, and according to his rank they assign him a chamber and bedding. During the month after the Rain-rest, the pious collec[illegible] united offering for the priesthood; and the priests in their turn hold a great assembly and preach the Law. . . . When the priests have received their dues, the householders and Brahmins present them with all sorts of robes and other necessaries; and the priests also make one another offerings. And so, ever since the Lord Buddha passed away from the earth, the rules of conduct of the priesthood have been handed down without intermission."

India under the Guptas must have been a country of almost ideal prosperity; a king who could govern without resorting to capital punishment must have enjoyed unexampled power, for Asoka himself was unable to go as far as this. Few things in all history are more attractive than this peep into India's Golden Age, where the "Law of Piety" was actually carried into practice. At Pataliputra, again, Fa Hian found public hospitals[1] maintained by the local landowners, where relief was given to the sick and destitute. Medical attendance was provided free, together with supplies of such drugs, medical appliances, and comforts, as might be necessary. At Pataliputra, Fa Hian gazed with wonder on the deserted palace of the Maurya Emperors, which he declares to have been the work of "no mortal hands," but to have been constructed by the Genii at Asoka's request; each of them, he asserts, brought one of the huge granite blocks, four or five paces square, of which the walls were constructed. It is interesting to notice how soon the great Emperor had passed from the realm of history to that of myth: this was partly due to his reputation as a Buddhist saint, which quickly involved him in all sorts of improbable monkish legends in a country where historical facts were seldom, if ever, recorded,[2] and partly to his genius for building. Stone buildings were practically unknown in India before Asoka's days, and for many centuries after his death they were the exception rather than the rule, and hence his great palaces, stupas, monasteries and pillars quickly began to be regarded with superstitious awe. In Fa Hian's time the centre of gravity had tended to move from the ancient capital of the Mauryas in a westerly direction; the Gupta Emperors

[1] In this respect, as in many other points of practical charity, Buddhism has anticipated Christianity. See pp. 32–33 *n*.

[2] Compare the case of Charlemagne in the Middle Ages.

considered Ayodhya a more convenient place of residence, and the travellers found many of the cities of Magadha comparatively deserted. Buddhism, too, had begun to lose its exclusive hold, and Gaya, the once renowned place of pilgrimage, the spot where the Master had attained Bodhi, was a wild and desolate jungle. Kapilavastu, the Bethlehem of Buddhism, was in an equally forlorn condition, and the palace where Gautama spent his boyhood was in ruins.[1] Evidently pilgrims no longer flocked to these sacred spots as of yore. At the cave on the hill called the Vulture's Peak, where Gautama had often resided, Fa Hian offered flowers and incense, and he records how the intimate contact of a place where the Master had actually dwelt moved him to tears. He failed in an attempt to enter the Deccan highlands, though he appears to have gone as far as the wonderful Ellura Caves. These too were almost deserted; the neighbouring villagers were "heretics," who regarded the recluses dwelling within the cells as possessed of supernatural powers, for a legend had arisen that many came to visit the caves "flying through the air."[2] Returning to Pataliputra, Fa Hian was at last fortunate enough to acquire the manuscripts he sought; the task had been a difficult one, for much of the teaching of Gautama was, in accordance with Indian practice, preserved orally,

[1] In one of the ruined palaces was a *picture* of the Immaculate Conception, where the Buddha, riding on a white elephant, enters his mother's side. The reference is interesting for students of Indian painting.

[2] This faculty was especially attributed to the Arhat. Compare the power of "levitation" ascribed to St. Francis of Assisi and his disciples.

and not entrusted to writing. Here Fa Hian's mission ended, and he longed to see his native country once more. His solitary companion, the only member left of the little band which had set out from China nearly twelve years before, refused to go any further. "He was captivated with the decorum of the priests, their religious deportment, their unworldliness in the midst of temptation, all of which was in sad contrast to the meagre knowledge and unhappy condition of the Buddhist Order in China." And so he took the robe and remained behind, taking a vow and saying, "May I never, until I attain Buddhahood, be re-born in a frontier land." But Fa Hian, animated by the noble desire of bringing knowledge to his fellow-countrymen, pressed on alone. Reaching the country of Tamralipti at the mouth of the Hoogly, he tarried for two more years in a monastery there, copying manuscripts and taking casts of images, and then took ship for Ceylon. In that island, of course, he found Buddhism in a flourishing condition, and at Anuradhapura he saw the Sacred Tooth, and the branch of the Bodhi Tree planted by Asoka's brother. Both these venerable objects may be still inspected by the traveller; the Tooth is now at Kandy, but the Bo Tree flourishes as greenly as ever in its little shrine at the end of the Sacred Road, while all around the gaunt ruins of dagobas and palaces rise above the surrounding jungle. In Fa Hian's days these great buildings were in the height of their glory, their brazen roofs shining like gold, and their pillars and walls adorned with richly-chased silver. In one of them stood a Buddha of pure jasper, holding in his hand a pearl of unknown value. But the heart of the old pilgrim was very homesick. "He had been absent from the home of his fathers for many years: the manners of the people he met were strange, and the plants, trees, towns and people were quite unlike those of old times. His companions were some of them dead, and lying in the distant mountain-passes, and others had left him: to think upon the past was his only consolation." And so he grew sadder and sadder. One day he saw a merchant offering to the jasper image a Chinese fan of white taffeta, and at the sight of this reminder, he broke down and wept.

And so, hurrying to the coast, Fa Hian set out for China. But his adventures were not yet over. A few days out, the ship encountered a storm and sprang a leak, and much of the cargo was thrown overboard, including the pilgrim's begging-bowl. He was in terror lest his precious manuscripts might follow suit, but his prayers were heard, and they reached the coast of Java after ninety days at sea. Here Fa Hian had to wait for five months before he found a ship to take him on, and one cannot help regretting that he tells us so little about that country. Apparently the splendid Buddhist shrines at Borobudur were not yet built, for he says nothing of them; the island, he tells us, was in the hands of "Heretics and Brahmins." His adventures were not yet over, however; his second voyage was almost as disastrous as the first, for the ship was caught in a typhoon and blown clean out of her reckoning. The water began to run short,—they had been seventy days at sea, and provisions had only been taken aboard for fifty,—and some of the sailors began to cast suspicious eyes upon the monk, whom they looked upon as a kind of Jonah. A plot was made to maroon him on an adjacent reef, and that would have been the end of our pilgrim, had not a plucky officer, who was himself a Buddhist, and a constant protector of Fa Hian, threatened, if they did so, that he would hand them over to the authorities at the first Chinese port. "I will go straight to the King and tell him of your crime, and he, as you know, is a Buddhist. So, if you kill this monk, you had better kill me too." At these firm words, the sailors desisted, and at last land was sighted. The travellers landed, and Fa Hian slowly made his way home. He was too pious a Buddhist to boast of his achievements, and he declares that he only wrote his modest narrative "to satisfy the curiosity of numerous inquirers."

A little over two centuries had elapsed since Fa Hian had returned from his wanderings, when the call came to Hiuen Tsiang, a young Buddhist priest of the province of Ho-nan. Hiuen Tsiang, the "Master of the Law," as he was called on account of his deep learning, had long sought for correct copies of the Scriptures in China; but, alas, the manuscripts were rare and imperfect, and differed in many important points. And so the thought came to him, "Why should not I, like Fa Hian and Chi-yen, visit the land of India, and learn from the sages, and worship at the places where the Lord dwelt and taught?" The time, however, was an unpropitious one. The great Tai Tsung, the Emperor of China at the time, had issued an edict against travellers visiting India, and it was impossible to obtain the necessary passes for the purpose of crossing the frontier. But Hiuen Tsiang was not easily deterred from his purpose. He travelled quietly to Kwa Chan, a frontier town on the edge of the Gobi Desert, and prepared to set forth. The liberality of the Governor, who nobly destroyed an order to detain him, prevented his project from being frustrated at the outset, and the Master of the Law set out bravely. He was much encouraged at the commencement of his journey by meeting an old traveller, who sold him a horse, "lean and of a red colour, with a varnished saddle bound with iron." Now, before he started, a clairvoyant whom he had consulted had said to him, "Sir, you may go; the appearance of your person as you go is that of one riding an old red horse, thin and skinny; the saddle is varnished, and in front it is bound with iron." The Master was accompanied by a young man whom he had met at a temple in Kwa Chan, and who had volunteered to accompany him; and the two successfully avoided the fort guarding the ford over the Bulunghir river by crossing the stream higher up. The stream was low, and they made a rough bridge of branches and scrub. In the desert, however, the young disciple's conduct became so suspicious, that it was clear that he only awaited an opportunity to murder the Master and decamp with his property: on being detected, he turned back home, and left his companion to pursue his journey alone. Hiuen Tsiang plodded along wearily. Mirages arose before his eyes, and he was well-nigh overcome when he reached the first of the series of forts guarding the wells on the road. Here he narrowly escaped being shot in trying to elude the sentry; but he managed to persuade the officer in charge to allow him to proceed. In the same way he passed the second, third, and fourth posts; the fifth he had been warned to avoid, and this involved a wide detour. It was a terrible journey. At the outset his water-skin burst open, and the precious contents were lost. For four nights and five days he wandered, till at last the "lean red horse" collapsed, and both lay, apparently dying, in the burning sands. But a vision seemed to come to the pilgrim, urging him to press on, and he roused himself for a final effort, and lo! behind a ridge of sand they stumbled on a green oasis, with bubbling water and fresh grass. Much refreshed, man and beast pushed on to the desolate hamlet of Igu, where they found three old Chinese priests, who wept to meet a fellow-countryman after so many years of exile among the Turki nomads. Here Hiuen Tsiang fell in with the prince of a district called Kao-chang, who gave him an enthusiastic welcome; he proved, however, a serious hindrance to the Master of the Law, trying to detain him permanently, and insisting on his paying him a prolonged visit. After staying here over a month, Hiuen Tsiang was allowed to go, and made his way from town to town until he reached the foot of the Thian Shan Mountains. It was on the way to the mountains that he met a rival doctor, named Mokshagupta, whom he vanquished in a disputation carried out in true medieval fashion. Mokshagupta had roused the Master's wrath by speaking of the *Yoga S'astra* as heretical, as, no doubt, it would appear in the eyes of a follower of the earlier type of Buddhism; but in the controversy that ensued, he proved to be incapable of even quoting correctly from the Sacred Books, and ultimately retired in confusion. After this, the biographer naïvely adds, "If Mokshagupta met Hiuen Tsiang, he did not sit down, but spoke standing, as if in a great hurry to get on."

The mountain passes were now declared to be open, but it was early in the year, and the caravan to which the pilgrim had attached himself suffered terribly. Twelve of them died of cold, fell down crevasses, or perished in avalanches. After this, however, the journey was easier. A hospitable Turkish Khan sent an escort to accompany him to the Indian frontier, where he arrived in September, 630 A.D., having travelled from Tashkend to Balkh, and from Balkh through the Bamian Pass to Kabul. Here the traveller kept the Rain-rest, according to the ancient Buddhist rule, after a year's perilous and arduous travelling. When the monsoon had ended, he set out for Kashmir, travelling through the Gandhara districts, and worshipping at the numerous shrines which had been built there in the days of the great Kanishka. The remnants of hundreds of these stupas and monasteries, adorned with graceful Indo-Greek frescoes, which must have been a source of endless joy to the pilgrim, are still strewn about the Gandhara country; in those days they were far more numerous, and while still undamaged by time and the hands of invading hordes, they were doubtless a beautiful and moving sight. Hiuen Tsiang has, however, no eyes except for relics and wonders; of the ancient schools of Taxila, of the carved façades of the temples, or the beauties of Kashmir scenery, he says not a word, and the reader becomes wearied of relics by the peck, of miraculous skull-bones, and authentic begging-bowls of the Buddha. One adventure, however, which Hiuen Tsiang encountered is so remarkable that it must be narrated in detail. The story is so circumstantially told that the reader must draw his own conclusions; it seems to be difficult to doubt the veracity of the Master, or question the accuracy of the narrative.

At a certain lonely cave outside the little town of Dipankara, not far from where Jelalabad stands now, it was reported that a luminous vision of the Blessed One appeared at times to pious worshippers, and thither went the Master. After much inquiry at the town, a little boy guided him to a lonely farmhouse, where dwelt an old Brahmin who knew the road. As they toiled across the barren hills, they were assailed by dacoits, but the pilgrim's yellow robe and his fearless demeanour abashed them, and at last they entered a stony nullah, at the head of which the cavern loomed, gloomy and forbidding. Tradition said that formerly a dragon had dwelt there. But Hiuen Tsiang entered fearlessly, and kneeling down commenced to pray long and earnestly. Time passed, and the pilgrim was in despair, when suddenly on the wall appeared a great orb of light, as big as an alms-bowl. Filled with joy, Hiuen Tsiang vowed never to leave the spot unless the Vision were vouchsafed, when lo! the wondrous thing appeared. "Then, whilst the whole cave was brightened up with light, the Shadow of the Blessed One, of a shining white colour, appeared on the wall, as when the opening clouds suddenly reveal the Golden Mountain and its excellent indications. Bright were the divine lineaments of his face, and as the Master gazed in awe and reverence, he knew not how to compare the spectacle: the body of the Buddha and his robe were of a yellowish red colour, and from his knees upwards the distinguishing marks of his person were exceedingly glorious; but below, the lotus throne on which he sat was slightly obscured. On the left and right of the shadow and somewhat behind, were visible the shadows of the Bodhisattvas and the holy priests surrounding them.[1] Overcome with joy, the Master summoned six attendants to light a fire and offer incense, but when the fire was lit the Vision faded, to reappear in the darkness. It lasted "about half a mealtime," and of the attendants five saw it, but the sixth declared that he could see nothing.

Among other interesting places visited by the traveller was the monastery where the Chinese hostages had been detained by Kanishka (here Hiuen Tsiang successfully exorcized the demon which had prevented the priests from touching the temple treasures), and the magnificent stupa at Peshawar, from the ruins of which archæologists have lately extracted the wonderful Indo-Greek casket containing the relics of Gautama.

In Kashmir Hiuen Tsiang found a hearty welcome. This country, dedicated to the Church by Asoka and Kanishka, had been the scene of the Great Council in

[1] The details of this remarkable story are most circumstantial. Beal brutally suggests the Vision was due to a magic lantern! This is, of course, an anachronism. It is interesting to compare the account of Fa Hian. "Here Buddha left his shadow. At the distance of ten paces or so we see it distinctly, with marks and signs perfectly bright and clear. On going nearer or further off, we see it less and less distinctly." (*Fo-Kwo-Ki*, xiii.)

the reign of the latter monarch, and in its numerous monasteries were many copies of the Sacred Texts and commentaries upon them, which could not be found elsewhere. Here the Master settled down for two years of study.

Early in 633 A.D., Hiuen Tsiang set out for Eastern India, the actual scene of the life of Gautama. He travelled in a very leisurely fashion, stopping at any monastery where he found priests or manuscripts likely to throw light upon obscure points of doctrine: the hospitality which awaits the mendicant all over the East made the life a pleasant one, and Hiuen Tsiang's reputation, ability in dispute, and venerable appearance gained him a ready welcome. In this way he reached Kanauj, the capital of the great Harsha, who was at that time the paramount sovereign of Hindustan. Hiuen Tsiang was destined afterwards to make the acquaintance of this monarch more fully: for the present he stayed at the city for a few months only. He gives us, however, a fascinating glimpse into the life of India of the seventh century, which may be instructively compared with what Fa Hian says about the land as he found it two centuries before. It is interesting to notice how little the Hindu has really changed, in spite of the lapse of centuries and the incursions of invading hordes. "The towns," he tells us, "Are walled: the streets are tortuous and winding. The houses and the town walls are built of mud and plaster on foundations of wood and bamboo: the houses have balconies, which are made of wood, with a coating of lime or mortar, and covered with tiles." This description explains why, except in a few exceptional cases, so little of the buildings of early India has survived. "The people's clothes are not cut or fashioned: they mostly affect fresh white garments: they esteem little those of mixed colour or ornamented. The men wind their garments round their middle, then gather them under the armpits, and let them fall across the body, hanging to the right." "The Kshattriyas and Brahmins are cleanly and wholesome in their dress, and they live in a homely and frugal way. There are rich merchants who deal in gold trinkets and so on. They mostly go bare-footed; few wear sandals. They stain their teeth red or black; they bind up their hair and pierce their ears. They are very particular in their personal cleanliness. All wash before eating: they never use food left over from a former meal. Wooden and stone vessels must be destroyed after use: metal ones must be well polished and rubbed. After eating they cleanse their mouths with a willow stick, and wash their hands and mouths." Of the morals of the people and the administration of justice the picture is equally pleasing. "With respect to the ordinary people, although they are naturally light-minded, yet they are upright and honourable. In money matters they are without craft, and in administering justice they are considerate. They dread the retribution of another state of existence, and make light of the things of the present world. They are not deceitful or treacherous in their conduct and are faithful to their oaths and promises. In their rules of government there is remarkable rectitude, while in their behaviour there is much gentleness and sweetness. With respect to criminals and rebels, these are few in number, and only occasionally troublesome. When the laws are broken or the power of the ruler violated, then the matter is clearly sifted and the offenders punished. There is no infliction of corporal punishment; they are simply left to live and die, and are not counted among men. When the rules of morality or justice have been violated, or a man is dishonest or wanting in filial love, his nose or ears are cut off and he is expelled from the city to wander in the jungle till he dies. For other faults besides these, a small fine is exacted in lieu of punishment. In investigating crimes, the rod is not used to extort proofs of guilt. In questioning the accused, if he answers frankly, his punishment is proportioned accordingly, but if he obstinately denies his fault, in order to probe the truth to the bottom, trial by ordeal is resorted to." Hiuen Tsiang then goes on to describe the curious ordeals to which the prisoner was subjected; they were neither more nor less foolish than those employed in Europe in the Middle Ages. For instance, the accused was placed in a sack tied by a long cord to a stone vessel, and thrown into the river. If the man sank and the vessel floated, he was guilty; but if the vessel sank and the man floated, he was innocent.

The system of government and taxation in vogue in India made a deep impression on Hiuen Tsiang; the executive, like the law courts, compared very favourably with the cruel and oppressive methods of his own countrymen. "As the administration of the government is founded on benign principles, the executive is simple. The families are not entered on registers, and the people are not subjected to forced labour. The crown-lands are divided into four parts. The first is for carrying out the affairs of state; the second, for paying the ministers and officers of the crown; the third, for rewarding men of genius; the fourth, for giving alms to religious communities. In this way, the taxes on the people are light, and the services required of them are moderate. Every one keeps his worldly goods in peace, and all till the soil for their subsistence. Those who cultivate the royal estates pay a sixth part of the produce as tribute. The merchants who engage in commerce travel to and fro in pursuit of their calling. Rivers and toll-bars are opened for travellers on payment of a small sum. When the public works require it, labour is exacted but paid for. The payment is in strict proportion to the work done."

Of the army we learn interesting details. "The military guard the frontiers and put down disturbances. They mount guard at night round the palace. The soldiers are levied according to the requirements of the service; they are promised certain salaries and publicly enrolled." The army was divided into infantry, cavalry, chariots and elephants.[1] The commanding officer, like the Homeric hero, rode in a chariot drawn by four horses abreast, his body-guard around him and a charioteer at either hand. The elephants wore armour plate; the infantry, like the Greek hoplites, depended chiefly on their long spears and large shields. The army advanced protected by a cavalry screen.

Comparatively little money circulated in the country. Ministers were often assigned lands for their support, and payment in kind, or by means of

[1] The recognized divisions, *pattakâya*, *as'vakâya*, *rathakâya*, and *hastikâya*.

the jewels and minerals of the country, was preferred to coin. The traders on the coast, of course, used coins, which were issued freely by the imperial mint; but coinage was a foreign invention, adopted, after Alexander, from the Bactrian Greeks and the Roman traders, and India is a conservative country. Even now, in the Indian bazaars, the poorer classes purchase their frugal requirements in minute quantities whose worth is more easily estimated in cowries than in coin.[1]

Hiuen Tsiang was struck with the immense fertility of North-Western India. Fruits of all kinds grew in abundance, and rice and corn were plentiful. It is quite possible that the Panjab was actually more fertile in those days than it has been since. The deflection of the monsoon current has, we know from Sir Aurel Stein's explorations, changed the once flourishing kingdom of Khotan into a sand-swept desert. Hiuen Tsiang says nothing about irrigation; hence we conclude that the crops grew naturally. The staple food at that time consisted of milk, butter, sugar, and wheaten cakes. It is significant to notice that animal food was no longer prohibited; fish, mutton, and venison, fresh or salted, were consumed, though certain animals, such as dogs, wolves, lions, and swine, were only eaten by the Pariahs. Beef was forbidden, and the universal superstition about onions and garlic made them taboo among the respectable classes. In these regulations we may detect sure signs of the decay of Buddhism; in the time of Fa Hian no animals were slain for food. Wine, too, was drunk by the Kshattriyas and Vaisyas, though not by Brahmins or

[1] See p. 64 *n*.

Buddhist monks. Caste-regulations, too, were becoming stricter; promiscuous inter-marriage, and the re-marriage of widows, were forbidden.

Of the religious sects of the time, with their bitter contentions, their philosophical theories, and their great monastic colleges, where learning was disseminated to all students who chose to attend, Hiuen Tsiang speaks from experience. Buddhism, long favoured by the Royal courts, was now beginning to decline, and the Brahmins were striving fiercely to regain their traditional position in the State. Buddhism, too, was torn by factions; the rival sects of the Greater and Lesser Vehicles lost no opportunity for attacking and reviling one another, and altogether there were eighteen schools, each with its separate leader. "Their contending utterances," says Hiuen Tsiang, "Rise like the angry waves of the sea." "In various directions," he adds, "They aim at one end. All, according to their class, gain knowledge of the doctrine of the Blessed One. But," he concludes sadly, "It is so long since the Lord lived on earth, that His doctrine is presented in a corrupt form, and so it is understood, rightly or not, according to the intelligence of the inquirer." The monasteries excited our traveller's admiration. "They are built," he says, "With extraordinary skill. A three-storied tower rises at each of the four angles, and the beams and projecting heads are carved into different shapes. The doors, windows, and wainscots are decorated with paintings;[1] the cells are plain on the outside and ornamented within. In the middle of the building is a high, wide hall." The subjects taught in the

[1] Another interesting reference to early Indian painting.

curriculum were grammar, mechanics, medicine, logic, and psychology,[1] and pupils often remained with their teachers from their seventh to their thirtieth year. "Then at last," we are told, "Their character is formed and their knowledge is ripe." Learning has always received due recognition in India, and many, though possessed of great wealth, devoted their lives to study. "Some," says Hiuen Tsiang, "Deeply versed in classic lore, devote themselves to study, and live a simple life apart from the world. Their names spread far and wide, and rulers invite them to court. The kings honour them on account of their gifts, and the people extol their fame and render them homage." As in the medieval universities of Europe,[2] the merits of the student were judged by his skill in argument. This is how Hiuen Tsiang describes a debate as he had himself often witnessed it in the great hall of countless colleges at Taxila, Nalanda, and other Buddhist centres of learning. Picture the scene—the long hall, dimly lighted with the Indian sun; the rows of silent, shaven monks squatting cross-legged on the floor, their saffron robes, draped so as to leave the left shoulder bare, lending a touch of colour to the sombre group; the President on his dais; and the eager disputants, expounding, according to the rules of Indian logic, some abstruse text of

[1] The five *Vidyâs*, *S'abda*, *Silpa*, *Chiktisa*, *Hetu*, and *Adhyâtma-Vidyâ*. Compare the "Trivium" and "Quadrivium" of the medieval European University.

[2] "Disputations" took the place of examinations in the medieval university. The candidate had to argue for his degree with a professor. He was greeted, according to his merits, with the formula "*optime*, *bene*, or *satis disputasti*." The disputation was not quite extinct in Oxford as late as 1834.

Buddhist metaphysic. "When a man's renown has reached a high distinction, he convokes an assembly for discussion. He judges of the talent or otherwise of those who take part in it, and if one of the assembly distinguishes himself by refined language, subtle investigation, deep penetration, and severe logic, he is mounted on an elephant covered with precious ornaments, and conducted by a retinue of admirers to the gate of the monastery. If, on the contrary, one of the members breaks down in his argument, or uses inelegant phrases, or violates a rule in logic, they daub him with mud and cast him into a ditch." Monastic discipline was strict. "The pursuit of pleasure belongs to the worldly life, the pursuit of knowledge to the religious life. To return to a secular career after taking up religion is considered disgraceful. For breaking the rules of the community the transgressor is publicly rebuked; for a slight fault he is condemned to enforced silence; for a graver fault he is expelled. Those who are thus expelled for life wander about the roads finding no place of refuge; sometimes they resume their former occupation."

In one respect the condition of India was less satisfactory than it had been in the days of Fa Hian. It was beset with dacoits, whom the government was apparently unable to control. Hiuen Tsiang several times suffered at their hands, but on the occasion which we are about to relate, he almost lost his life. He had set out from Kanauj for Benares by one of the numerous passenger boats which plied at that time along the Ganges, and they were passing through a dense forest of asoka trees which overhung the banks for miles on either hand. Suddenly a swarm of pirate vessels darted out of the bushes, boarded the ship, and towed it to the bank, where the ruffians proceeded to strip and plunder their unfortunate captives. Now it happened that these pirates were worshippers of the goddess Durga, like the Thugs of later days, and they were accustomed every autumn to offer a human victim to that deity, in order to assure a prosperous season. When they saw the Master of the Law, they selected him as a worthy victim, and in spite of the prayers of the passengers, many of whom offered to die in his place, they seized him and carried him off to a flowering glade hard by, where they bound him and laid him upon an altar. The hideous rites were about to begin, when the Master asked for a few minutes' respite, and begged his murderers "Not to crowd round him painfully, in order that he might compose himself, and prepare to depart with a calm mind." Then the Master prayed long and earnestly to the Maitreya Buddha that he might be re-born in the Tushita Paradise, and learn from his blessed lips the Yoga S'astra which he was destined not to study on earth, and the sound of the excellent Law. Lastly, he prayed for his murderers, and asked that when he had perfected himself in wisdom, he might be re-born on earth in order to instruct and convert them, and thus to give peace to others by spreading the benefits of the Law." And then, as the Master meditated, he seemed to fall into a deep trance, and to pass into the Maitreya's presence, "Amid the excellently precious adornments of heaven, with companies of angels upon every side." And now a strange thing happened. One of the fierce sand-storms so common in Central India suddenly broke upon the company, filling the air with dust, and lashing the rivers into waves. The superstitious robbers, frightened by the omen, desisted from the sacrifice, and gazed in an awestruck manner upon their victim, while the passengers, seizing their opportunity, warned them what calamities they would bring upon themselves if they laid hands upon the great saint from China. The brigands were so overcome that they knelt before Hiuen Tsiang, and one of them touched his hand by accident and awoke him from his trance. The Master looked up and said, "Has the hour come?" But when he saw what had happened, he preached to them of the sin of robbery and impious sacrifices. "How can you," he said, "Risk the woes of ages for the sake of this body, which is as transitory as the lightning flash or the dew of the morning?" The robbers restored all the property which they had looted, threw the instruments of their worship into the river, and allowed the passengers to proceed on their journey. This circumstance added greatly to the Master's fame.

We need not follow Hiuen Tsiang in his various visits to the sacred spots associated with the life of Gautama: he found them even more ruinous than they had been in the time of Fa Hian: and at last he arrived at that most holy of places in Buddhist eyes—the Bodhi Tree at Gaya. At the sight of the tree, and the other objects connected so intimately with the life of the Buddha, Hiuen Tsiang was overcome with emotion, and kneeling before the beautiful image in the temple, reputed on account of its great loveliness to have been carved by Maitreya himself, he prayed, saying, "At the time when Buddha attained wisdom,

I know not how I was, in the troubled whirl of life and death: but now, in these latter days when men have only images to worship, reflecting on the load of evil which I have done, I am filled with sorrow." Here Hiuen Tsiang met some priests who took him to the temple of Nalanda, where the great saint Silabhadra dwelt. Silabhadra is said to have been warned in a vision of the coming of a disciple from China, and for two years Hiuen Tsiang dwelt with him, learning of the mysteries of the Yoga S'astra, for which he had sought so long. And here a curious thing happened. One day Silabhadra was giving a public lecture to Hiuen Tsiang and others, when a certain Brahmin in the audience began to laugh and cry in a hysterical fashion. And when they asked him why he behaved thus, he said: "I am a man of Eastern India. And once I prayed to the image of Avalokiteswara to make me a king. But the Bodhisattwa reproved me in a vision, saying, 'Pray not thus; hereafter shalt thou hear the saint Silabhadra expound the Yoga S'astra for the sake of a priest from China: from hearing this discourse thou shalt be able hereafter to see the Buddha, what then is the use of wishing to be a king?' And now, behold, I have seen the priest of China come, and the Master for his sake expounding the law. Therefore I laugh and cry at the wonder of it."

Hiuen Tsiang gives us a vivid picture of the beauties of the famous Nalanda college and monastery, which is of especial interest, as we know so little of medieval university life in India. The Buddhist monk always chose for his home a place with pleasant and cheerful surroundings, unlike the gloomy Indian ascetic, who haunted grave-yards and performed repulsive penances. "The whole establishment is surrounded by a brick wall. One gate opens into the great college, from which are separated eight other halls, standing in the centre of the quadrangle. The richly-carved towers and fairy-like minarets cluster like pointed hill-tops; the upper storeys and observatories are lost in the morning mists. From the windows one sees the wind wreathing the clouds into various shapes, and from the soaring eaves one may observe the conjunction of the planets. Down below, the deep, transparent ponds bear on their surfaces the blue lotus, mingled with Kanaka flowers, of a deep red colour; at intervals the Amra groves throw a grateful shade over everything. All the outside courts, in which are the priests' chambers, are of four stages. The stages have carved and coloured eaves, pillars and balustrades, and the tiled roof reflects the light in a thousand shades." The lecture rooms were about one hundred in number, and often the number of residents amounted to ten thousand. Yet the students were earnest and grave, and breaches of the rules were practically unknown. As in medieval monasteries in England, the necessaries of life—rice, butter, and milk—were supplied by neighbouring villages.[1]

From Nalanda, the Master of the Law set out on a very extended tour through India. The details do not concern us greatly, but he appears to have gone as far south as Amravati, where he gathered many details about Ceylon, and thence in a north-westerly direction through the Deccan, perhaps to Nasik, the

[1] Compare Fa Hian's account, *Fo-Kwo-Ki*, xvi.

headquarters of the Maratha King Pulikesin II.[1] He appears to have visited the Ajanta Caves on the way. Of the Marathas he speaks highly; they were brave and upright, and had defeated all who tried to penetrate into their fastnesses; but the pilgrim adds that their courage had a very "Dutch" element about it, men and elephants being supplied with strong drink upon the eve of a battle. Perhaps this curious story was invented by the soldiers of Siladitya to account for their defeats. From Nasik the pilgrim travelled through Broach and Kathiawar, and into Sind; he then turned eastwards and once more reached the Nalanda monastery. His studies were now nearly completed, and his thoughts were turning towards home, when an imploring message from Kumara, King of Assam, induced him to go upon a mission to preach in that country. Kumara had heard how a wretched "Heretic" had nailed a paper containing "Forty unanswerable theses" upon the monastery gate, and how the Master had torn it down and trampled on it, and in a public disputation pulverized the challenger in the presense of his followers; the prince added, that if the Master did not come speedily, "As sure as the sun was in heaven, he would send his elephants to stamp Nalanda into dust." But Kumara was not allowed to retain his acquisition long. The news reached the ears of his overlord Siladitya, who ordered the Chinese priest to be sent to him at once. Kumara

[1] The difficulty of penetrating into the Deccan was proverbial. "The country of the Deccan," says Fa Hian, "is precipitous, and the roads dangerous. Those who wish to go there have to bribe the king, who gives them guides. These guides pass the travellers on from one locality to another, the men of each locality alone knowing its bypaths and passes." (*Fo-Kwo-Ki.*, xxv.)

replied they might have his head, but not his priest; but the prompt appearance of a royal envoy with the message, "Then I trouble you for your head," induced him to alter his mind without further ado. So Kumara and Hiuen Tsiang travelled up the Ganges with a gorgeous retinue, and Siladitya met them amid the beating of golden drums and the blaze of torches. The whole party marched in state to Kanauj, where splendid religious ceremonies were held, lasting for nineteen days, in which the King and his vassals rode on elephants, escorting a golden statue of Buddha, which had been made at great cost as an offering for the monastery. Here Hiuen Tsiang expounded the Mahayanist doctrines to the assembled court. Among the audience was the King's widowed sister, for in pre-Mahommedan days women in India enjoyed freedom and enlightenment. They received the same education as men, and often chose their own husbands. *Sati* was a voluntary act of devotion, and was probably uncommon when the widow was not forced to undergo the degradation later inflicted upon her, and when she had intellectual diversions to occupy her mind. So great did the Master's reputation become, that no one dared to take up the challenge which he hung to the door of the assembly room, even though he offered his head as a recompense "To any-one who should prove a word of his arguments to be contrary to reason." Perhaps this reluctance was party due to an order of the King, that if any one spoke against his protégé, his tongue should be torn out by the roots!

This lavish patronage bestowed upon a foreigner and a Buddhist, aroused intense jealousy in the numerous religious sects which haunted the precincts of the court, and more than once attempts were made to assassinate both Siladitya and Hiuen Tsiang. The King was attacked on one occasion by a fanatical Brahmin, who all but stabbed him; and the culprit confessed to a plot among his fellow-conspirators to set fire to the edifice in which he was watching the ceremonies. These plots were the beginning of the long struggle which ended in the overthrow of Buddhism by the Brahmins. After the celebrations at Kanauj, Hiuen Tsiang was taken to see a great distribution of charitable gifts at Allahabad, or Prayaga, as it was then called. On the sands at the junction of the Ganges and Jumna a vast throng of beggars, ascetics, Brahmins, *sanyasis*, and the like, such as only India can produce, had assembled. For nearly three months they were fêted by the King, who distributed among them the accumulated wealth of five years, down to his own jewels and embroidered robes. And so ended the strangest scene in Hiuen Tsiang's varied adventures among the peoples of India.

And now the pilgrim was determined to set out for China. With the greatest difficulty he persuaded his royal host to release him, and at last he departed, having refused all the gifts lavished upon him except a fur-lined cloak to enable him to face the icy cold of the mountain-passes. He travelled leisurely to the north of the Panjab, crossed the Pamirs, and reached Khotan late in 644 A.D. His journey had not been without its trials, for he had lost some books owing to a squall while crossing the Indus, and some more when he was attacked by brigands and an elephant had stampeded. But the treasures he had brought were unparalleled in quantity and value—caskets full of relics, wondrous statues in gold, silver, sandal-wood and crystal; and, above all, no less than six hundred and fifty-seven volumes of Indian manuscripts. The permission to return to China was gladly given, and the pilgrim's journey from the frontier to the capital was a long triumphal procession. His record was, indeed, unique; for seventeen years he had travelled and studied; he had faced countless perils, in the sandy, burning deserts, on the icy and impenetrable mountains, and among the robbers and brigands of many countries; he had seen the place where the Blessed One was born, and the Bodhi Tree where He obtained knowledge for the saving of the world. But worldly honours and rewards meant nothing to the Master of the Law. Retiring to a monastery, he set himself down to translate the Sacred Books for the benefit of his countrymen, and to lecture to all who wished to hear upon the sciences which he had acquired in India. It is pleasant to learn that, ten years after his return, a deputation of Indian monks from the Mahabodhi Temple made the toilsome journey to China in order to visit him. In 661 A.D., the Master, being now sixty-five, began to feel symptoms which warned him that his work on earth was approaching its end. He had finished seventy-four works, in thirteen hundred chapters, besides many copies of sutras, and drawings. An old malady, originally contracted when crossing the mountains, attacked him with increasing violence. And so, on the thirteenth day of the tenth month of the year 664 A.D., repeating some verses in adoration of the

Maitreya, he passed peacefully away, earnestly desiring to be re-born in the Paradise of the Lord of Love. Here he waits until, in the fulness of time, the Maitreya shall again take human form, and then Hiuen Tsiang will return to preach once more the Law of Piety to his fellow-creatures.

V

IBN BATUTA.

V

IBN BATUTA.

1304–1378 A.D.

> "For always wandering with a hungry heart,
> Much have I seen and known, cities of men
> And manners, climates, councils, governments."

Of all the ancient travellers, few can boast of a record approaching that of the jovial Moor, Ibn Batuta. His appetite for wandering was perfectly insatiable. He was travelling continuously for over thirty years, and is estimated to have covered, during that period, over seventy-five thousand miles. He explored Asia Minor, visited Constantinople and Russia, and journeyed far north to investigate the phenomenon of the midnight sun; he sailed down the African coast to satisfy his curiosity about Mombasa and Zanzibar; he performed the *Haj* four times; he made the overland journey to India, where he won the favour of that eccentric sovereign Mahommed Taghlak, and was appointed a judge at Delhi; he went from Delhi to China on an embassy, visiting Ceylon, Java and Sumatra *en route;* and not satisfied with this, on his return home he undertook a long and perilous trip to Central Africa, which anticipated by centuries the achievements of the greatest African explorers.

And yet Ibn Batuta was no hero. His motives were neither pious nor disinterested. He travelled chiefly because he liked variety, excitement, and opportunities of studying his fellow-men; and doubtless, a pilgrimage to Mecca, or a journey through Persia to India with a caravan, afforded a shrewd student of human nature the same opportunities for amusement and observation which similar excursions in the Christian world would give to Ibn Batuta's great contemporary, the genial author of the *Canterbury Tales*. The hazards of the way were less than might be expected; though Ibn Batuta occasionally found himself in a perilous position, he usually appears to have travelled leisurely and comfortably, and that wonderful freemasonry which made a Mahommedan welcome from Gibraltar to Canton ensured him a hearty reception wherever Islam prevailed. No doubt, too, Ibn Batuta's own plausible manner, his knowledge of men, and his marvellous stories of the countries he had visited made him popular with his hosts all over the world.

When Ibn Batuta started on his travels in the year 1325 A.D., Mahommedanism was the foremost power in the world. In two continents out of the three then discovered, Islam held undisputed sway; Asia Minor, Persia, Arabia and India were ruled by Mahommedans, and the religion was spreading to China and the Malay Peninsula. All the known parts of Africa were under Mahommedan rulers, and the brilliant Arab astronomers and chemists were laying the foundations of modern science. Even Europe for a time was seriously threatened with the danger of being overpowered by a great Pan-Islamic incursion; Spain and Sicily, indeed, were recaptured, but the defeat of the Crusaders had been a serious blow, and the Turks were already casting envious eyes on the decrepit Byzantine Empire. Mahommedan Khans ruled in Southern Russia, and it was only the heroic efforts of the Papacy and the Italian States which prevented them from becoming supreme in the Mediterranean basin.

Ibn Batuta started his travels by a journey from Tangier to Cairo. From here he went to Palestine. After visiting the tombs of the Patriarchs, and also Bethlehem, Jerusalem, and various other localities of religious interest, he accomplished the main object of the expedition by setting out for Mecca. Among the many places at which he stopped, one of the most striking was Meshed-Ali, the Arabian Lourdes. Here cripples from all over the world assembled on a certain day, and at sunset were laid upon the tomb of the martyr Ali. "People then, some praying, others reciting the Kuran, and others prostrating themselves, wait expecting their recovery. About nightfall they all spring up cured." Our traveller did not actually witness the "Night of the Revival," though he knew many trustworthy persons who had done so. From Arabia he travelled to Persia, and visited Ispahan and Shiraz, ultimately returning to Baghdad. Shortly afterwards, he determined to perform the *Haj* again, and this time he stayed for three years at Mecca Prolonged sojourn at one place, however, was not to his taste; and very shortly afterwards we find him on a voyage down the East Coast of Africa. He touched at Aden, where he noticed the great water-tanks, and also stopped at Mombasa and Zanzibar.

He makes many shrewd remarks about the flora and fauna of the coast, and was much struck by the commercial possibilities of the cocoa-nut palm. Among many good stories which he narrates, one of the most amusing relates to a certain holy Shaikh, who was attacked by divers heretics who rejected the doctrine of predestination. "You believe in free will," said the Shaikh, making some passes in the air. "Very good, move from here if you can." The wretched men found that they were hypnotized, and had to sit, unable to stir hand or foot, all day long in the burning sun! In the evening the Shaikh brought them round, and dismissed them, sadder but wiser.

From the African coast, Ibn Batuta sailed to the Persian Gulf to watch the pearl-fisheries. He then travelled across Arabia, paid a third visit to Mecca (1332 A.D.), and tried to get a boat to take him to India. Failing to do this, he crossed the Red Sea, travelled overland to the Nile (a most perilous enterprise) and worked his way upstream to Cairo. After a brief rest, we find him travelling in the Levant, after which he took ship across the Black Sea to Russia, and paid a visit to the great Uzbeck Khan, who ruled over the Mahommedan Mongols on the Volga. Here Ibn Batuta was amazed at the shortness of the northern nights. It was Ramadan, and to his surprise he had hardly time to finish the sunset prayer before midnight; while, hurry as he might, he was overtaken by the dawn, half-way through his midnight devotions. Ibn Batuta was soon after entrusted with an errand very much to his liking. A Greek princess, who had married a Mahommedan Khan, was returning on a visit to her parents at

Constantinople, and the gallant traveller was asked to escort her. At Constantinople he was well received by the Emperor (Andronicus I.), who was interested in the traveller's account of the sacred sites in the Holy Land (remembered, no doubt, "with advantages," by Ibn Batuta), but the sentries scowled and muttered "Saracen! Saracen!" as they presented arms to the *cortège* entering the gate. Ibn Batuta describes at great length the marvellous city, a living relic of the long-passed ancient world, with its palaces, churches, monasteries, and works of art. He little thought that in just over a century's time it would be in the hands of his co-religionists. He was vexed by the incessant ringing of the church bells, a strange and discordant sound to the Eastern ear.

The traveller now determined to go farther afield. It was probably easy to find in an emporium like Byzantium merchants bound for India; at any rate Ibn Batuta attached himself to a caravan which was setting out for India by the overland route *viâ* Balkh and the Kabul Pass. He reached the Panjab in the month of Moharram, 1333, after nearly perishing in the defiles of the Hindu Kush. He is the first writer to give these mountains (anciently called the Paropamisus, or Hindu Caucasus), their modern name. It means, he says, "Hindu Slayer," and was bestowed because very few Hindu captives, carried off by the Mongolian raiders, ever survived the horrors of the journey. What a wealth of unrecorded suffering lies hidden behind this grim title! At Delhi Ibn Batuta's plausible tongue quite won over the Emperor Mahommed Taghlak, who made him a judge on a salary of twelve thousand rupees a year, together with a handsome *inam*. Here he stayed eight years, and he tells us a good deal about India at that period. Amongst other things he saw *Yogis*, who performed the rope trick, and could raise themselves in the air, and was so overcome by their marvels that he nearly fainted. He hints that they mesmerized their audience in some way. A prolonged stay in one place, however, ill accorded with Ibn Batuta's temperament; he was over fifty thousand rupees in debt, and was engaged in some extremely dangerous intrigues. He was glad, therefore, to get an offer from the Emperor to go upon an embassy to China, and set off in great pomp in 1342. India was not a safe country for travellers where the Moghul law did not run, and the journey to Calicut was highly adventurous. Worse, however, was to follow, for the boat containing the gifts for the Chinese Emperor was swamped soon after starting. Ibn Batuta thought it would not be prudent to return with this tale to Delhi (where he had not left behind the best of reputations), so he decided to start life afresh. After a few desultory changes, he took a boat for the Maldive Islands, where he found, as he hoped, an untrodden field for enterprise. Here he soon ingratiated himself, and settled down for a year among the shady palm-groves. He married four wives of the country, and became a judge; but the spirit of wandering was strong within him, and in 1344 (divorcing his wives on the plea that they would not stand travel) he set out for Ceylon. His wanderings in Ceylon are a little obscure, but he tells the usual travellers' tales about monkeys, moonstones, and venomous leeches. The most interesting portion of this part of the story is his visit to the famous

"Footmark of our Father Adam." Ibn Batuta climbed the mountain by the more precipitous route, and with his usual accuracy of detail noticed the chains erected to help pilgrims at precipitous places, and the masses of scarlet rhododendron on the lower reaches.

From Ceylon he went to Southern India, and stayed at Madura. After a series of adventures he reached Chittagong, where in pursuance of his original plan, he took a boat for China. On the way he landed at Sumatra, and gives a very poor account of the inhabitants. In China he found the reigning monarch to be a descendant of Jengiz Khan. He was much struck with the industries of the Chinese, especially their porcelain. He also noticed their skill with the pencil. On returning to a town previously visited, he found the walls decorated with admirable caricatures of himself and his companions! One curious adventure happened to him in China. One day he saw a man staring at him intently, and found him to be a fellow countryman who had also been at Delhi, and the meeting affected both to tears. Strange to say, Ibn Batuta met his brother, years after, in the heart of the Soudan. On his way home, Ibn Batuta and his shipmates were terribly scared by an apparition which they thought was the formidable Roc, well known to readers of the *Arabian Nights*. However, it vanished harmlessly, and was probably a mirage. Landing at Arabia, Ibn Batuta performed the *Haj* for the fourth and last time, and reached home at the end of 1349. Here he found that his father had died fifteen years before. In 1352 he once more set out, this time for Central Africa, and succeeded in reaching Timbuctu, and the Niger, which he mistook for the Nile. In 1354 he returned, convinced by his travels that there was "no place like home," after all.

Evidently a life of hardship did not hurt the old adventurer, for he lived over twenty years more, and died at the ripe age of seventy-three, after dictating his memoirs to the king's secretary. No one will quarrel with the note at the end of the Arabian manuscript which declares that "No sensible man can fail to see that this Shaikh is the Traveller of our age; and it would not exceed the truth were we to call him 'The Traveller of Islam.'"

VI

AKBAR.

VI

AKBAR.

1556–1605 A.D.

Heresy to the Heretic, Religion to the Orthodox,
But the rose-petal's dust for the heart of the perfume-seller.

ABUL FAZL.

HARDLY anything in history affords more painful reading than the story of the Mahommedan incursions into India. A wild and brutal race of fanatics, entirely unprovoked, makes a series of inroads into a prosperous, civilized, and well-governed country. Like the Spaniards in America, they burn, plunder, and massacre, and return laden with spoil, excusing their crimes under the cloak of religion. The stories of the sack of Somnath, or of the five-day massacre of the Hindus at Delhi, when Timur, not content with slaying ten thousand prisoners in cold blood, left the streets impassable with the heaps of corpses of unoffending citizens, are only too typical of the events of those cruel days. The only consolation is to be found in the reflection that India, to some extent, merited her fate; wealth and ease had brought weakness and indolence in their train, and that fatal lack of union, the besetting sin of India from the beginning of time, allowed her various defenders to be conquered in detail. It was the same in the days of Alexander. The invaders—though this in no way palliates their horrid cruelties—won because they deserved to.

With the coming of the Moghuls, however, a new era dawns in Mahommedan history. With Babar we seem to come upon different ground. Poet, knight-errant, and adventurer, Babar has, for some reason or other, hardly a trace in his nature of the wild ancestry to which he belonged. Few men have ever had a tithe of the adventures which were crowded into his brief but meteoric career. Succeeding at the age of twelve to the throne of Ferghana, three years later he conquered Samarcand, the birthplace of Timur. Driven out of Samarcand, he was still hardly more than a boy when he seized the kingdom of Kabul. Not content with Kabul, he was tempted, in 1526, to follow his predecessors in the congenial pastime of raiding the Panjab. Beating the Mahommedans at Panipat in the same year, and the Rajputs at Agra in the next, he died in 1530, under fifty, but ruler of an empire which stretched from the Ganges to the Oxus. His son, the brilliant, reckless Humayun—*capax imperii nisi imperasset,* as the Roman historian would have said—spent a troubled twenty-six years in alternately beating his numerous foes and being beaten by them. After at one time flying through the desert for his life, he returned in triumph, only to die from a fall on the marble steps of his palace in 1556.

Such was the parentage of Akbar. Born while his father was a fugitive in the wilds of Sind, he passed a wild and adventurous childhood. Yet, though it

THE TAJ MAHAL.

(Photo by the Author.)

[*To face page* 107.

fitted the boy for coping with the thousand and one dangers which beset him who dared to aspire in those days to the throne of Delhi, it did not debase or brutalize him. Akbar was filled with the kindly humour, the grace, the sense of the poetry of life, which flashes out on every page of his grandfather's memoirs, and which shines in every line of the tombs and palaces of his graceless grandson. The line of Babar was a race of poets; the Taj Mahal, most glorious of shrines, is an epitome of their aspirations, their achievements, and their failings. Akbar was almost as young as his grandfather when his career began. He was barely fourteen when the news of his father's death reached him, but he had already seen fighting, under the tutelage of his guardian, Bairam Khan.

For a moment it seemed as if the Emperor's demise must ring the death-knell of Moghul aspirations in India; the revolting Afghans, led by an able Hindu adventurer named Hemu, swept all before them, and it was expected that the boy-king would soon be flying once more for his life across the deserts. But Akbar was made of sterner stuff than this. He and Bairam rallied their forces for a final effort; Bairam cut down with his own sword the officer who had surrendered Delhi; and this sobered the rest. By a clever dash, the Moghuls captured the whole of the enemy's artillery, and then advancing to the historic field of Panipat, where India has three times been lost and won, beat them in a well-contested fight. Hemu, shot in the eye, was brought a prisoner to where Akbar and his staff were standing. "Try your sword on him," said Bairam; and when Akbar indignantly refused to strike a wounded man, he despatched the wretched prisoner himself, with a sneer at the lad's squeamishness. But Akbar was not so docile as he appeared to be. Bairam, the Bismarck of his age, thought that he could rule as he liked, and treated the young Emperor with good-humoured contempt, raising his own *protégés* to power, and punishing sternly all who interfered. To his astonishment, Akbar, collecting his adherents under the pretence of a hunting party, declared the great Minister deposed. Bairam, at first incredulous, and then inclined to ridicule the idea of the possibility of Akbar's getting on without him, finally lost his temper and rebelled. But he had few friends, and he was quickly compelled to sue for pardon at the feet of his former pupil. Akbar, with a magnanimity rare in those days, freely forgave him and sent him off to Mecca on a pilgrimage—an honourable form of banishment, or rather ostracism, often imposed upon a dangerous rival. Bairam never reached the holy place. An assassin—one of the many victims of his days of power—stabbed him at the port of embarkation.

And now Akbar, aged eighteen, found himself alone, and almost immediately he began to inaugurate the policy of forming a united India, which will be to all time the chief glory of his name. He recognized that the great curse of the country was disunion; Hindu and Mahommedan were at variance, and hardly less bitter was the strife between Shia and Sunni, Turk, Afghan and Moghul. Above all, Akbar's heart went out to the Rajputs; he had heard, no doubt, warriors who had fought under his grandfather at Panipat, tell how the "Sons of Kings" had charged the Moghul guns till the blood dyed their horses' chests; and how Sanga Rana, their leader, "Carried more than eighty wounds from sword or lance; an eye destroyed by an arrow, an arm lost in a fight with Ibraim Lodi, and a leg smashed by a cannon shot." Could not these people be reconciled to the throne? Akbar meant to try. The first step was taken when he married the daughter of Raja Bihari Mal, Lord of Amber, and the second, when he remitted for good the two taxes which pressed heaviest of all upon Hindu pride and Hindu pockets—the pilgrim-tax, and the *jizia*, or commutation money. The latter, above all, was a hated imposition, a sign of servitude; for the Kuran laid down that all infidels should be put to the sword, and it was only by favour of the conqueror that they were allowed to redeem themselves at a price. After this, only one Rajput state ventured to withstand the Moghul Empire. The Rana of Chitor bade defiance to the invader, and for months he withstood all attempts to capture his stronghold. Finally, however, Akbar stormed the town, after himself killing the brave commandant with a lucky shot from his favourite carbine. But the House of Udaipur, though beaten, was unsubdued; the survivors fled to the hills and held out there, and to this day they boast that they alone dishonoured their race by no union with the unbeliever. Two other expeditions followed—one to Ahmedabad, to bring Gujarat to obedience, and one to the refractory province of Bengal; and Akbar settled down to the peaceful task of reorganizing his Empire upon the novel lines which he had initiated already. Kasim Khan erected the fort at Agra, with its massive battlements of red sandstone, two miles in circumference and seventy feet in height; and soon afterwards the City of Victory, Fathpur Sikri, was built by the Emperor round the dwelling of the saint Salim Chishti, the birthplace of Prince Salim, the beloved son whom the Rajput Princess bore him. We have seen how Akbar had won over Hindu and Rajput by his just policy. He now introduced the system of promotion by merit, irrespective of caste or creed; and Hindu officers began to hold posts, civil and military, in great numbers. One of these, Raja Todar Mal, became Akbar's *Wazir*, and started the great financial reforms which were ever afterwards adopted as the basis of systems of taxation in India. The system of tax-farming, with all its innumerable train of evils, was abolished; the land was re-surveyed and re-assessed, and it was arranged that the tax should be on the crop rather than the soil, in order to minimize the hardships of drought and famine; money was freely advanced to encourage agriculture; and the evils attendant upon the presence of a royal or official camp in a district (even now often made an excuse for extortion by subordinates, and in those days of immense retinues simply ruinous to the villagers), were minimized by strict regulations and fixed tariffs. India is a poor country, and most of her woes are financial. Akbar's scheme did incalculable good, in spite of the comical charge of Badaoni, who hated all infidels and heretics with a deadly loathing, that "many a good Mussalman perished beneath the pincers of Birbal and his fellow-extortioners." Among Akbar's humane enactments were laws against *sati*[1] and child-marriage, and other social regulations, relaxing the stern ordinances of the Shastras and the Kuran, and making the conscience of the individual, rather than State compulsion, the standard of right and wrong.

But Akbar went further than this. He realized that the chief obstacle to union was a religious one. Religious bigotry, then as now, presented an insuperable bar betwixt ruler and ruled. And yet were not all religions at heart one? Akbar had come into contact with the Hindu religion through his Rajput wife; he had watched her perform her daily devotions in the chapel of her palace, and he had discovered, as many of us have yet to discover, that Hinduism was neither a monstrous nor an immoral creed. The Sufi of Persia taught a form of Pantheism which was not very different from the Vedanta, of which, through translations, the Court was beginning to hear a great deal. The Sufi (Σοφοί, Enlightened[2]) were, perhaps, a survival of the Gnostics of early Persia, and so were a connecting link between Mahommedan, Christian, and Buddhistic beliefs. And the similarity between Mahommedanism and Christianity was evident. And so Akbar assembled at Fathpur Sikri doctors of all creeds, and tried to arrive at a common basis upon which a universal religion might be

[1] The widow was to do what she wished, to be dissuaded but not forced. Often the unfortunate woman was hurried, drugged, to the fire by scheming relatives or priests. For the other aspect of *Sati*, see Coomaraswamy's translation of the *Sûz-u-Gudâz* (London, 1912).

[2] I take the derivation from Keene. It is far more reasonable than the one ordinarily given.

founded. Great was the rage of the orthodox Mahommedans. His policy was denounced from every pulpit, and as no one dared attack the Emperor in person, the brunt of their wrath fell upon his chosen friends, Faizi and Àbul Fazl. "They led His Majesty from Islam," says Badaoni. Akbar only laughed. Often the debates lasted till dawn, and nothing amused the Emperor more than when some one scored neatly off an angry Maulvi in an argument. "What will they say of this at Constantinople?" cried a champion of orthodoxy, in despair, at the Emperor's latest heresy. "If you like Constantinople so much you had better go there," retorted Akbar, significantly. Most of all, Akbar patronized the plucky Jesuit priest, Father Rudolfo, whose black cassock soon became a familiar figure at Court. The Emperor was strangely drawn by the new creed from the West, though it is doubtful whether he would ever have become an orthodox Christian. Certainly he would never have become an advocate of proselytizing on its part. Akbar's aim was a different one. He sought

> "To gather here and there
> From each fair plant, the blossom choicest grown,
> To wreathe a crown, not only for the king,
> But in due time for every Mussulman,
> Brahmin and Buddhist, Christian and Parsee,
> Through all the warring world of Hindustan."

Perhaps Akbar's feelings on the subject have never been so well expressed as in the famous lines written by Abul Fazl, and destined, it is said, to be inscribed upon the walls of a temple in Kashmir :—

O God, in every temple I see people that seek Thee: in every language I hear spoken, people praise Thee.

Polytheism and Islam feel after Thee: each says, Thou art One, without a second.

If it be a Mosque, men murmur the holy prayer: if it be a Church, they ring the bells from love of Thee.

Sometimes I frequent the cloister, sometimes the Mosque: but Thee I seek from Temple to Temple.

Thine elect have no dealings with heresy or orthodoxy: neither stands behind the screen of Thy Truth.

Heresy to the heretic, Orthodoxy to the orthodox. But the Rose-petal's dust belongs to the Perfume-seller's heart.

"The Rose-petal's dust to the Perfume-seller's heart!" Few, alas, were found to agree with Akbar's mighty dream. The time had not come. It has not come yet. To orthodox Mahommedans it was abhorrent; to the laxer sort it was made an excuse for looseness of living. Padre Rudolpho would have been the last to accept it; nor would the better class of Hindu.[1] When Akbar asked Man Singh whether he would join him in the new creed, "Sire," said the young warrior, "If loyalty means readiness to sacrifice one's life, I trust I have given your majesty proof of my fidelity. (He was thinking of that day in Gujarat when he, his father, and the Emperor were cut off in a narrow lane by the rebel cavalry, and the three cut their way through in a glorious charge.) But I was born a Hindu. Your Majesty would not have me a Mahommedan. And I know no third religion." But opposition merely strengthened Akbar's determination, and he crushed orthodox contumacy by declaring himself head of the Church. Finally, he ratified this decision by himself addressing the people in the courtyard of the great Mosque. It is not difficult to picture the scene. In front stands

[1] Raja Birbal was the only Hindu of rank who joined.

the great crowd: the bright March sun lights up the glittering uniforms, the many-coloured turbans, the gleaming marble canopy of the Saint. Akbar, a simple figure in a white robe, only ornamented with a single gigantic diamond—the Koh-i-nor, gift of the house of Gwalior—in his aigrette, mounts the pulpit beneath the aisle. He begins to intone the solemn litany composed by Faizi :—

> "The Lord to me the Kingdom gave,
> He made me prudent, strong, and brave,
> He guided me with right and ruth,
> Filling my heart with love of truth,
> No tongue of man can sum His state,
> Allahu Akbar! God is great."[1]

But as Akbar began to chant the great hymn, his emotions overwhelmed him. He saw, in his mind's eye, a united India, a race untorn by religious controversy or racial prejudice. "One fold and one shepherd." It was too much. He faltered, stopped, broke down utterly, and abruptly left the pulpit. The awed crowd remained in respectful silence until the service was taken up by a member of the courtly circle and finished.

And so, for many happy years, life passed at the Court of Fathpur Sikri. The country was enjoying a period of peace and good-government unknown since the Mahommedans first passed the Indus. To the Emperor it was a time of unalloyed happiness. Absorbed in his social and financial reforms, his mechanical experiments—for Akbar, like his grandfather, was keenly interested in such matters, and

[1] Keene's translation, *History of Hindustan*, p. 114.

had devised many improvements in firearms—his religious debates, and his building schemes, his life was spent in congenial and absorbing occupations. At his side stood his Rajput kin, most loyal of friends, Faizi and Abul Fazl, whom he loved, perhaps, better than any one in the world, and Raja Birbal, the merry troubadour and brave soldier. Discussions in the Debating Hall, we are told, often lasted till sunrise, and the dawn was welcomed by a choir singing a hymn to the Sun, while the kettle-drums sounded in the *Nakkar Khana*—the Musicians' Balcony—over the gateway. Then the King would take his seat on the throne of the Hall of Audience with his nobles round him, receiving petitions, hearing the complaints of all, from the highest to the lowest, and welcoming ambassadors and foreign visitors. Then, perhaps, would follow a review, when the cavalry, the elephants, and the artillery would defile past the Presence. The King knew every detail of his soldiers' equipment; he was well aware that upon the instant readiness of the Household Brigade depended his throne, perhaps his life. After this followed private consultations and audiences in the Council Chamber, and then His Majesty withdrew to his private apartments, for the Moghuls, who were never really acclimatized to the heat of Northern India, wisely worked late at night and early in the morning, reserving the midday for sleep. As the evening drew on, the Court would retire to the polo-ground, where the game was prolonged even after the dusk had set in, by means of balls coated with phosphorescent paint; or perhaps bull-fights or elephant-fights were the order of the day. When the Court moved to Agra these were held in the moat, the ladies, in their fluttering, many-coloured silks, peeping cautiously from the marble-screened battlements at the scene below, or gazing idly on the Imperial flotilla which cruised on the waters of the silver Jumna. A favourite amusement of Akbar's was the game of *pachisi*, or backgammon, played with living pieces in the courtyard, while the spectators sat round and watched.

But this state of things was too good to last. Akbar had now been king for thirty years, and uninterrupted peace was a thing unknown in India. The first blow came when Birbal, like many a good officer since, fell in a disastrous little war on the Frontier. In 1595 Faizi died, and with the loss of two out of three of his chosen friends Akbar was broken-hearted. A severe famine did not mend things; and some incompetent blunders on the part of Prince Murad involved the empire in a war with the Deccan. For a time, however, the "Emperor's Fortune" prevailed. Ahmadnagar, bravely defended by Chand Bibi, its gallant queen, until her murder, was stormed; so was Asirgad, where the silly young Raja of Khandesh had taken refuge. Returning home, Akbar built his famous Triumphal Arch, the *Buland Darawaza*, beside which the Arch of Titus shrinks into insignificance. As the traveller enters, two inscriptions meet his eye on the walls of the portico. The one on the left resembles in its grand simplicity the noble words of the Behistun Rock. "His Majesty: Lord of Lords: enthroned in Heaven: shadow of God: Jalal-ud-din: Mahommed Akbar: Emperor! I conquered the Deccan and Dandesh, which men called Khandesh, in the year of the Divine

Faith 46, which is the *Hijri* year 1010."[1] On the right, Akbar the man, weary and disillusioned, warns us of the transitoriness of mortal things. "Jesus said: *The world is a bridge; pass over it, but build no house thereon.*[2] Who hopes for an hour, hopes for eternity. The world is an hour; spend it in prayer, for what follows is unseen." The words are prophetic, ominous of coming trouble. Two years later came the crowning blow of Akbar's life. An indulgent father, he was cursed with dissolute and idle sons. Daniyal died of drink; but even more bitter was the disappointment caused by Salim, the beloved son, the child of many prayers, born of Akbar's union with the Rajput lady, and destined, as his father fondly hoped, to unite in his person Mahommedan and Hindu. But he had the virtues of neither, the vices of both. Cruel, capricious and dissolute, he was too fickle, or too cowardly, even to conduct a successful campaign. He was bitterly jealous of Abul Fazl, whom he suspected of warning the Emperor about his evil courses, and in a fit of passion he hired some dacoits to set on the minister and murder him. It was a heartless act. Akbar, though he refused to believe that his son actually instigated the deed—he was mercifully spared this blow—knew that he approved of it. "If he wanted the crown, he should have taken me," he said. And from that day he pined and sank. He saw with dismay that his schemes would die with him: his temper became violent and uncertain, and he who was famed

[1] *I.e.* 1600 A.D. One of Akbar's innovations was to redate the calendar from his accession. He renamed Khandesh "Dandesh," after Prince Daniyal.

[2] An apocryphal saying, preserved in Mahommedan tradition.

for his clemency, began to perpetrate acts as cruel and arbitrary as those of his ancestors. He hurled a wretched servant, whom he caught sleeping, out of a window. He died from a fit of passion brought on by a quarrel between the retainers of his son and grandson. And so, overburdened by his load, he passed away after forty-nine years upon the throne of Delhi. To the end he clung desperately to the hope that Salim might reform, and his last act was to order him to be invested with the royal robes. Dreams are evil things for the dreamer.

VII

SHIVAJI THE MARATHA.

VII

SHIVAJI THE MARATHA.

When, in the distant ages, the Aryans began to push on beyond the Panjab, southwards and eastwards, in search of new homes, they found upon their right a vast plateau, the approaches to which were guarded by broad rivers, thick jungles, and steep, densely-wooded hills. Into this wild land Aryan civilization penetrated scantily and slowly. In the epic story of the Ramayana we may detect a reminiscence of the early struggles of the invaders against the aboriginal "demons" of the forests. And all through the præ-Mahommedan period the hardy highlanders of the Deccan, the South Country as it was vaguely called, retained their independence. The great Asoka was content with sending missionaries to the Rastikas.[1] They resisted the encroachments of the medieval Hindu emperors. Hiuen Tsiang, the Chinese traveller, found it impossible to penetrate the wild tangle of ravine and jungle which confronted him on the borders. The Deccan has been compared

[1] The word "Maratha" means the "Maha Rattas," the Great Rattas, or Rastikas, an early tribe who once held the Deccan. The Canarese Raddis are a remnant of the tribe. The derivation from Maha-Rastra, the "great country," *par excellence*, flatters local conceit, but is quite meaningless.

to the Scottish highlands. In some respects the comparison is not a bad one. In both countries the stern, barren mountain tracts, where a man must work hard and live frugally, or starve, have produced a hardy, active race, wiry and brave, and inspired with an intense love of the wild hills of their native land.

Τρηχεῖ' ἀλλ' ἀγαθὴ κουρότροφος is as true of the Maharashtra as it was of ancient Ithaca. One feature of the country has played an overwhelming part in its history. The action of the fierce monsoon rains upon the mountain ridges has carved out numbers of bare, flat-topped peaks, easily convertible, by means of a few bastions and curtains at the least inaccessible points, into almost impregnable fortresses. From immemorial times the Maratha hillmen have made use of these natural strongholds, fleeing to them when attacked, only to sally forth again upon the retiring foe, and to hang upon his flanks like a pack of hungry wolves. In the more level country the Maratha commonly rode a pony as small and hardy as himself. A perfect horseman, he was more than a match over the rough ground of the Deccan, for the heavy cavalry of Hindu or Mahommedan invaders from the northern plains. One is reminded, when reading of the fruitless endeavours of Aurangzeb to bring the Marathas to an open engagement, of the English campaigns against Wallace and the Bruce in Scotland. Indeed, Froissart's description of the Scottish army applies admirably to the Marathas. "It consisted of twenty thousand men, bold and hardy, armed after the manner of their country, and mounted upon little hackneys that are never tied up or dressed, but turned immediately after the day's march to pasture on the heath or in the fields. They bring no carriages with them on account of the mountains they have to pass, neither do they carry with them any provisions of bread or wine, for their habits of sobriety are such that in time of war they will live for a long time on flesh half-sodden without bread, and drink the river-water without wine. . . . Under the flap of his saddle each man carries a broad piece of metal, behind him a little bag of oatmeal; when they have eaten too much of the flesh, and their stomach appears weak and empty, they set this plate over the fire, knead the meal with water, and when the plate is hot, put a little of the paste upon it, and bake a thin cake like a biscuit, which they eat to warm their stomachs. It is, therefore, no wonder that they perform a longer day's march than other soldiers." The Maratha warrior, even more frugal than the Scot, often subsisted for several days upon the ripe corn of the country, which he plucked and rubbed between his hands as he sat upon his horse.[1] This, and a draught of milk begged at the nearest village, was enough to satisfy his wants.

The Marathas, however, were unable to resist the great Mahommedan invasion which penetrated right down to Cape Comorin in the early years of the fourteenth century. The Deccan, though not in the true sense of the word conquered, became part of the Empire of Ala-ud-din. A few years later, Zafar Khan, the governor, rebelled, and set up an independent monarchy, which, following the law of

[1] Grant Duff, vol. i., note, p. 571 (end).

Oriental states, eventually split up into five portions, of which by far the most important were the kingdoms of Bijapur in the south, and Ahmednagar in the north. These two kingdoms practically divided the Maharashtra between them. We need not follow in detail the confused struggles which occupied the Mahommedan kingdoms of the Deccan for the next two centuries. In 1565 Bijapur vanquished and overthrew the great Hindu Kingdom of Vijayanagar; in 1571 she combined with Ahmednagar in a fruitless attempt to dislodge the Portuguese. In both kingdoms the number of Mahommedans are comparatively small. Adventurers from Abyssinia, Persia, and Turkey certainly found their way to the capitals from time to time, but not in sufficient numbers to form an army large enough to hold the country. The Mahommedan rulers were forced to employ Hindus very extensively, both in civil and military posts; they were at best a small garrison, confined to the principal towns, with here and there a Mahommedan officer in charge of a detached post at a fort or other strategic point. These latter, cut off from their companions, and living a lonely life in a hostile country, generally neglected their duties, and the forts more often than not were in a ruinous condition, hopelessly undermanned, and carelessly guarded. By far the larger part of the Deccan was held in fief by the great Maratha nobles, who, like the feudal barons of medieval Europe, were allowed to do practically as they liked in their estates, in return for military service. Their forces were of such magnitude as to render their services indispensable, and this made them still more independent.

PRATAPGAD FORT.

[*To face page* 125.

About 1586 a new factor was introduced into Deccan politics; the Kingdom of Ahmednagar was reduced to a state of anarchy by the quarrels of the Mahommedan and Hindu factions, and the Hindu party committed the fatal error of soliciting the help of the Moghuls from Delhi. As is usually the case, the intruders, once called in, were not easily got rid of; the Emperor Akbar, perceiving the weakness of the Mahommedan states in Southern India, conceived the idea of annexing them. Too late the Kingdom of Ahmednagar made desperate efforts to repel the invader. The heroic Chand Bibi,[1] the widowed queen, fought hand-to-hand in the breaches until she fell, the victim of a particularly loathsome intrigue. After her death, Malik Amber continued the struggle with varying fortunes till 1626. In these wars the Maratha nobility played a considerable part. The desertion of Lakhoji Jadhavrao to the Moghuls in 1621 practically settled the fate of Ahmednagar; another Maratha chief, Shahji Bhonsle, after going over to the Moghuls, and trying his hand at a little king-making of his own, decided, about 1637, to leave Ahmednagar to its fate, and to enter the service of the still flourishing monarchy of Bijapur. Shahji Bhonsle was an ambitious, and not over-scrupulous, soldier of fortune. Married by his father to the daughter of Jadhavrao, the first noble in the Deccan, he quickly rose to prominence as a military officer. His son, Shivaji, was born in 1627, and shared in his

[1] The great women of Indian History, both Mahommedan and Hindu—Sita, Damayanti, Chand Bibi, Ahilyabai, and countless others, down to that grand old rebel, the Rani of Jhansi—sadly belie the traditional "down-trodden Indian woman" of the story-books.

youth the adventures inseparable from his father's calling. The parents do not appear to have agreed very well; the difference in rank between them was a source of friction, and after the treaty of 1637 Shahji took another wife, and went off on a long campaign in the Carnatic, leaving Jijibai and her child by themselves in his family estate of Poona. Here young Shivaji grew up under his mother's influence. Most Hindu women are conservative. Jijibai was no exception to the rule. Proud, bigoted, and intensely religious, she brought up her son in accordance with the most orthodox traditions. He early learnt to regard with hatred the Mahommedans as the enemies of his country and his gods, to reverence the Hindu religion and the Brahmins, and to love the romantic legends of the mythical heroes of India, and the saints and deities of the Maharashtra. Poona has always been a place of peculiar sanctity, a stronghold of Brahminism, and Shivaji imbibed its atmosphere from his very youth. What he needed of practical training he acquired from his guardian, Dadoji Kondadev, the administrator of Shahji's Poona estate; he could neither read nor write, for these were arts proper to the Brahmin, not to the soldier; but his love of the national songs of the land was sufficiently shown when one day he risked his life by stealing right into his enemies' camp to hear a recitation by a rhapsodist, of the kind that are still popular among the Marathas. His patron saint was the goddess Bhavani, the consort of Shiva in her most terrific aspect; his chaplain or spiritual director was Ramadas, a celebrated saint and poet of no mean order. For the most part, Shivaji had been allowed from his boyhood to run wild among the mountains which cover a large portion of his father's estate. Here he became the close companion of the Mavlis or highlanders of the district, who taught the young chief to ride and shoot, and use the sword and spear. They took him hunting and climbing until he grew to know every nook and cranny of the hills; and, what was more, he gained an almost incredible influence among the men of the hills, who soon declared themselves ready to follow him anywhere.

As Shivaji grew up, he could not fail to perceive what an excellent chance was offered for a bold adventurer to declare for independence in the Maharashtra. The Bijapur Government, two hundred miles away, cared little what happened in these barren hills, provided that the tax-farmers sent their scanty tribute with tolerable regularity. Their armies were busy in the Carnatic, and the Mahommedan lords, in their luxurious palaces, considered the poor, half-savage Marathas scarcely worthy a thought. And so, when Shivaji sent a messenger to say that he had captured the hill-fort of Torna, no one greatly cared, especially as the emissary promised that his master would pay a far larger rent than the former holders. A few judicious bribes settled the matter. One by one, Singad, Purandhar, and other fortresses followed suit. Still the authorities did nothing. At last Shivaji grew bolder; he seized the Governor of Kalyan by a clever stratagem, and made himself owner of that important district, with its fine harbours and fertile territory. This act at last roused even Mahommed Adil Shah, and he tried to coerce the young recreant by seizing his father as a hostage. For the next four years Shivaji's actions were hampered by fear of retaliation. He corresponded with the Moghul Emperor, Shahjahan, at Delhi, and threatened to call him in, which kept the Bijapur authorities from taking active steps, till finally, in 1657, they decided to release their old officer, whose help they needed owing to fresh complications in the Carnatic. But no sooner was his father out of danger, than Shivaji started upon his adventures again. The Raja of Javli, a powerful nobleman, had resisted all inducements to join in the rebellion, and a plot was formed to make an end of him once and for all.[1] Bodies of Mavlis were concealed in the thick jungle on the borders of his town. Two of Shivaji's officers then entered, pretending to have come with a message from their master. They treacherously stabbed the Raja in open court, and escaping in the tumult which ensued, raised the signal for the Mavlis to issue forth from their ambuscade. In spite of a brave resistance, the retainers of Javli were soon cut down, and the territory passed to Shivaji. Historians who enlarge upon the enormity of the crime forget the temper of the age and the necessities of the situation. The feeling between the Morés and Shivaji was of the bitterest kind, and he only behaved exactly as any of his opponents would have done to him under similar circumstances. Shivaji was naturally neither treacherous nor cruel; but as an outlaw bent upon a desperate career, he carried his life in his hands.

[1] Besides this, he must have been privy to Baji Shamraji's plot to seize Shivaji in Javli territory and hand him over to Bijapur. There is no doubt what would have happened to Shivaji in that case.

Neither Moghul, Adil Shah, nor his own neighbours would have shown him any mercy if they had caught him. It was a question who should strike first.

About two miles from the scene of this tragedy stands an abrupt, almost conical hill, since named Pratapgad. The scenery around is wild and beautiful in the extreme. On the east tower the huge, scarped cliffs of the Mahableshwar range, the home of the "Great Strong God," where the sacred Krishna sets forth on its long journey to the Bay of Bengal. To the west, the land slopes away down to the level plains; on the horizon may be dimly discerned the faint, silver line of the distant sea. On all sides, the summit is guarded by sheer precipices; far below, dense masses of tropical jungle make the country impassable to all but the highlanders of the districts, whose little hamlets, clustering in tiny clearings along the course of the mountain streams, may be perceived here and there. The position was of immense strategical importance to Shivaji. It commanded the recently conquered district. What was more important, it dominated the Par Pass, the great highway between the Deccan highlands and the fertile fields and flourishing ports of the Konkan.[1] Here Baji Shamraj had lain in wait for Shivaji at the beginning of his career, only failing by his own faintheartedness to nip the great warrior's career in the bud. It was therefore only natural that Shivaji should immediately seize the rock and detail his famous Brahmin officer, Moré Tirmal Pinglé, to put it in a state of defence. The Bijapur Government, agitated by the internal

[1] There are now two other roads, the Kumbharli and Fitzgerald roads.

troubles which ensued on the death of Mahommed Adil Shah at the end of 1656, and threatened with a fresh Moghul invasion by the young Aurangzeb, still looked on inertly; their armies were sufficiently occupied in keeping order among the rich zamindars of the Carnatic, and they heeded little what happened in the barren mountains of the Deccan, which scarcely repaid the cost of occupation. Shivaji no sooner heard of the proposed expedition from Delhi, than, with his usual adroitness, he began to make terms with Aurangzeb. As soon, however, as the latter was recalled by political complications nearer home, he plundered the territory of Ahmednagar, penetrating up to the walls of the city itself. He returned home laden with spoil, driving in front of his men hundreds of captured horses, which he sadly needed as cavalry remounts. A raid like this, defying openly the cherished foe of their race, and offering unlimited opportunities of loot, was dear to the Maratha heart, and enormously increased Shivaji's reputation.

The next year (1659) Shivaji sent a large force to invade the Konkan, the rich country lying between the Ghats and the sea. The coasting ports, with their important pilgrim - traffic to Mecca, were threatened; the loss of the allegiance of the local chiefs to Bijapur seemed imminent, and the Maratha foragers penetrated right into the Kolhapur district, almost to the borders of Bijapur itself.

At last the Government was aroused. They had, by their incredible supineness, allowed a formidable rebellion to grow up, which a few years earlier might have been stamped out by a few hundred men in a week. This time, however, they determined that no mistake should be made. A force of twelve thousand troops, cavalry and infantry, with rocket batteries and mountain guns on camel-back, was despatched under the command of an experienced Pathan officer named Afzul Khan, who knew the Deccan well, having held a post some years before in the neighbouring district of Wai. Before his departure, Afzul Khan boasted in open Durbar that he would drag the "Mountain Rat" in chains to his sovereign's throne. The jest was an ill-omened one. Afzul Khan was *fey*, as the Scotch would have said. To make things worse, he desecrated on his way the famous temples of Bhavani at Tuljapur, and of Vithoba at Pandharpur. No Maratha would henceforth show him mercy, least of all Shivaji, who had a brother's life and the honour of his goddess to avenge.

Shivaji, on the news of the enemies' approach, retreated to the new fortress at the head of the Par Pass.[1] As the Mahommedans toiled wearily along the winding road, their commander no longer took the same hopeful view of the situation. On both sides the steep, jungle-clad hills rose abruptly, their summits clothed in dense mist. At any moment the force might find itself ambushed in a position where superior numbers would avail little. The cold rain disheartened and wearied the men, and no one looked forward to the escalade of an almost impregnable fortress, preceded, perhaps, by an arduous and dangerous siege. On the other hand, Shivaji's position was far from enviable. He dared not meet his opponents in the open field, and if he were shut up for long in his stronghold, his power over the

[1] Early in October, 1659.

country would vanish as quickly as it had arisen. The rival chiefs of the Deccan, always ready to join the winning side, would desert him, and the work of years would be undone. He therefore sent messengers to his opponents, imploring them to parley. Afzul Khan assented gladly, and despatched a Brahmin officer of the name of Gopinathpant, with a suitable retinue, to arrange terms of peace agreeable to both parties. The ambassadors were hospitably received; and that night Shivaji secretly visited the Brahmin's tent, and implored him to aid the cause of his country and her gods. Blood is thicker than water. Gopinathpant at last consented, and it was agreed that an interview between the leaders should be arranged. To this Afzul Khan raised no objection; probably he thought that he would find an opportunity to assassinate or capture his foe. Himself a man of huge stature, and skilled in the use of arms, he saw nothing to fear in an open meeting with the insignificant Maratha. Shivaji's attitude was very different. The night before the interview he spent in prayer before the image of his goddess, and rising before dawn, he performed with the utmost scrupulousness the elaborate ablutions prescribed by his religion. He dressed with great care. Beneath his long linen robe was a coat of the finest chain-armour; in his belt was the famous Bhavani sword, and concealed in the palm of his left hand lay the terrible Tiger's claws, sharp steel hooks fastened to the fingers. Kneeling at the feet of his mother, he asked her blessing, and then he bade his friends farewell, and committed his little son to their care in case he fell.

The fatal morning had arrived. The Mahommedan

force had already moved to the village of Javli, the scene of the tragedy five years before; and now the Khan, seated in a litter and accompanied by an escort of fifteen hundred cavalry, advanced to the interview. At the foot of the fort the troops halted and dismounted, while Afzul Khan, accompanied by a single officer, went forward along the winding path leading to the stronghold. As he came in sight, Shivaji, accompanied by his tried comrade Tanaji Malusré, came down to meet him. What exactly happened after this, we shall never know. Afzul Khan may or may not have struck the first blow; but Shivaji, leaning forward as if to embrace him, thrust the Tiger's claws into his entrails. In another moment, his sword was knocked out of his hand and he was cut down. His companion, who to his lasting honour refused the generously offered quarter, had no chance against the famous swordsmanship of the Maratha leaders. In a moment, he, too, fell; and the preconcerted firing of five guns from the fortress gave the signal for a simultaneous attack upon the troopers and the main force at Javli. With wild cries, the Mavlis rushed from their concealment upon the doomed army; the unfortunate troopers, caught dismounted and utterly off their guard, fell almost to a man; of the main body many surrendered, and were treated with the utmost humanity—for Shivaji, a true soldier whatever his detractors may say, was always honourable in dealing with his prisoners. Others fled into the jungle, where they were quickly lost or devoured by the wolves and panthers of the hills. For many days, famished soldiers wandered in and gave themselves up.

Seldom has a battle been more decisive and more cheaply won. At a single blow, Shivaji had utterly destroyed a picked Mahommedan force, and had captured camels, elephants, specie and guns, to say nothing of over four thousand valuable horses. In order to follow up his victory, he immediately organized an expedition into the Carnatic. The strong forts of Rangana and Panhala, in the Kolhapur district, were taken, and the Marathas, plundering and burning, advanced almost to the gates of Bijapur. Unfortunately, however, on his return journey, Shivaji allowed himself to be invested in Panhala fort, from which, after a four months' siege, he only escaped by a somewhat ignominious ruse. Asking for a truce preparatory to surrender, he slipped out under cover of night, and joined a body of troops who were awaiting him. In the morning the Mahommedans, furious at the deception, followed in hot pursuit; it was on this occasion that the gallant Baji Prabhu saved his master's life at the expense of his own. Shivaji, with the enemy at his heels, reached a narrow pass in the Ghats; a few miles further and he would be safely inside the walls of Rangana; so, detaching this officer with a thousand Mavlis to hold it, he bade them not fall back until five guns were fired from the fort. It was another Thermopylæ. For nine hours the devoted band hurled back successive relays of fresh troops who charged up the defile; at last, just as the long-expected signal was given, their commander fell mortally wounded, and the heroic little force retired slowly to the fort, bearing their leader's body with them. They had lost three-quarters of their number, dead or wounded, in the engagement.

For the next two years (1661–1662), the Bijapur Government, realizing the hopelessness of conquering Shivaji, and undermined, as usual, by factions which deprived them of the services of their ablest leaders, appear to have granted him an informal truce. Shivaji, however, was not a man to rest upon his laurels. Having conquered the Deccan as far as Goa in the south, he proceeded to attempt to repeat his successes against the Moghuls in the north. He set out against Aurangabad, whilst his fleet, a new departure on his part, harassed the coasts, and held up the pilgrim-ships bound for Mecca, to the intense anger of the orthodox Aurangzeb. The Moghul commander, Shahiste Khan, who was sent to chastise the rebels, found he had no light task in front of him. At the outset, his whole force was checked by the obstinate defence of the fortress of Chakan, which cost him nine hundred men. Then, though he occupied Poona, he was unable to dislodge Shivaji from Singad, the gigantic rock-fortress overlooking the town. It was at this juncture that Shivaji performed one of those picturesque feats of gallantry by which he is remembered all over the Deccan. He and a few picked companions entered Poona in disguise in a wedding procession, and that night they raided the house of the commander-in-chief. Shahiste Khan only just escaped with his life; he jumped out of a window, receiving, as he did so, a sword-cut which deprived him of one of his fingers, and his son and many retainers were killed. Shivaji and his followers escaped in the darkness, and hastened back to their friends. All night long, the mortified Mahommedans saw torches and bonfires blazing on the sides of

Singad, and to make matters worse, a body of cavalry which rode out of the city to reconnoitre next morning, fell into an ambush and were chased ignominiously back.

In 1665, however, the great Rajput leader, the Raja Jayasingh of Jaypur, was sent to command operations in the Deccan. He laid siege to Purandar, and Shivaji, feeling that resistance was hopeless, came to terms with him at once. Shivaji was a prudent man; he knew his hillmen could cut up a small, ill-led force, storm a fort, or surprise a town, but the time had not come when the Marathas could defy the Great Moghul to his face. Giving up twenty of the Deccan forts, he offered to join an expedition against Bijapur, and then, having thoroughly ingratiated himself with the Moghul authorities, he boldly set out the following year for Delhi, to demand of Aurangzeb his acknowledgment as a feudatory of the empire. Shivaji, however, had reckoned without his host. Aurangzeb, cold and suspicious, received his overtures with indifference. To his dismay, he found himself practically a prisoner. There is little doubt that the Emperor intended eventually, upon some excuse or other, to make away with him, and then, after subduing the Deccan, to proceed to the conquest of the hated heretics of Bijapur. He had not forgotten Shivaji's raid upon Ahmednagar, nor, above all, his attacks on the pilgrim-boats bound for Mecca.

Shivaji viewed the situation with growing uneasiness. He asked to be dismissed on the ground that the climate injured the health of his followers. Aurangzeb, while gladly allowing the latter to return to their homes, refused permission to their leader. By a clever ruse, however, Shivaji managed at last to escape from his implacable foe: feigning sickness, he and his son were carried outside the town in one of the long wicker baskets, heaped with flowers and sweetmeats, in which it was the custom to despatch charitable gifts to the crowds thronging the courtyards of the mosques and temples. Once outside the town, they found a swift horse awaiting them, and on this they rode for dear life to the sacred city of Muttra. Here the great chief was hidden by a Brahmin family, and then, disguised as a *Yogi*,[1] he was quickly swallowed up in the vast crowds of pilgrims and devotees who resort to the spot. Soon afterwards he reappeared in the Deccan, to the immense joy of his people. The gallant Tanaji had arranged the plans for his master's escape, and no doubt the family of Jaysingh connived at it: for Jaysingh had guaranteed Shivaji's safety, and a Rajput never breaks his word.

The next two years were the most peaceful in Shavaji's life. Aurangzeb, having lost his victim, pretended that he had voluntarily dismissed him, and his old enemy, the King of Bijapur, actually consented to pay a considerable tribute to the once despised "Mountain Rat." These years of leisure were spent in organizing the country on an altogether new system, for Shivaji, like Napoleon, was a skilled administrator when he was given time to attend to such matters. The army was put upon a regular footing, well-paid and organized. It was no longer

[1] The favourite trick of the political suspect, practised both at the time of the Great Mutiny and to-day. It nearly always baffles the police.

an undisciplined band of hillmen : besides the Mavlis, Hetkaris, the skilful marksmen of the low country, and cavalry were enlisted. The forts received the greatest attention. They were carefully repaired, armed, and provisioned : each had a civil and military officer, with elaborate instructions for the posting of sentries, guards, and so forth. As their total number was nearly three hundred, the task of an invading army which ventured into this veritable wasp's nest was not likely to be an enviable one. The people of the lower castes, living at the foot of the fort, were given free lands on condition that they guarded it and supplied it with fodder and provisions. They were taught to regard the fortress "as their mother," and well and faithfully they performed their duties. They alone knew the forest paths; they watched the on-coming foe, warned the garrison of his approach, and harassed his flanks and rear. The civil administration was conducted by eight great officers of state, most of them veteran leaders of Shivaji's army : the Government was very decentralized, and as little interference as possible with the village officials, who governed in accordance with the immemorial, unwritten custom of the people, was allowed; justice was administered by the Panchayat, or Tribunal of Five, as it always has been in India. Here again the jury represented local tradition.

In matters of revenue Shivaji effected great and lasting reforms, based upon the principles taught him by his old tutor, and acquired ultimately from the system of Todar Mall, the minister of Akbar. The value of the land was not regarded as fixed; every year the crops were assessed, two-fifths of the amount being paid to the Government. The old system of tax-farming, with its horrible abuses, was utterly stamped out; all taxes were paid direct to the royal officer. And lastly, the feudal system of granting lands in fief, in return for service, was abolished. The soldiers were henceforth the servants of the Government, and not retainers of the local chiefs; and so the most fruitful cause of rebellion and disunion was removed. No offices, civil or military, were to be hereditary; merit alone was to earn them. Nor were Brahmins only employed; Marathas and Prabhus had their share of posts, and even the lower orders had definite duties assigned to them. By a mixture of castes, a check was put upon a species of oppression even now not unknown in India.

Shivaji, however, was not left long in peace to carry out these judicious reforms. Aurangzeb, treacherous as ever, had given orders that he should be secretly captured. The plot leaked out, and Shivaji at once declared war upon his dastardly opponent. Among the forts that had been surrendered to the Moghuls was the great castle of Singad, the Lion's Den, commanding the city of Poona, and at the time it was garrisoned by a Rajput regiment, under a famous officer named Udé Ban. Shivaji determined to recapture it. Thither, then, early in February, 1670, set out a body of one thousand Mavlis from Raigad, under the great Tanaji and his brother Suryaji. In order to avoid suspicion, they went by devious paths only known to themselves, and met at a rendezvous at the foot of the rock. It was a dark night, the 9th of February, moonless and bitterly cold. Above, the sentries, half-asleep, were cowering over their fires or in the corners of the ramparts, to avoid the chill winds which blow upon the Ghats in the winter. Choosing the least accessible side, where forty feet of sheer black rock towers above the hillside, Tanaji began to ascend. This part of the stronghold was weakly fortified and carelessly guarded, for it was deemed unscalable—as, indeed, it was to any but a Deccani highlander. How Tanaji climbed it in the dark, it is impossible to surmise. The feat was one of almost incredible difficulty. At last, however, the top was reached, and letting down a rope, Tanaji hauled up and made fast a ladder. Three hundred of the Mavlis had ascended, when a sentry took alarm. He was shot, but too late, by an arrow;[1] blue lights and flares showed to the garrison the little party of stormers on the cliff-side. Seeing that they were discovered, Tanaji ordered them to charge; but he fell in the onset, and the Marathas in dismay began to retreat. At that moment, however, Suryaji reached the summit with the reserves. Seeing what had happened, he rallied the force by telling them that the ladder was down, and there was no escape. "Cowards!" he cried, "will you leave your father's body to be tossed into a dung-pit by scavengers?" Stung by the taunt, the Marathas raised their war-cry, "Har, Har, Mahadeo!" and flung themselves like tigers upon the foe. The brave garrison, as the furious mass charged down upon them in the darkness, fell back inch by inch, till at last they could go no further. Many, disdaining to yield, flung themselves over the cliff and were dashed to pieces.

[1] One man in every ten carried a bow and arrow, as this weapon was useful for surprises, when a gun would give the alarm.

Resistance grew fainter and fainter, till at last it died out, and the Marathas fired a thatched hut to give the signal to the anxious watchers on the walls of Raigad. When the bleak dawn arose, a horrible sight met the eye. The fort was a shambles. The two commanders lay dead, with three hundred Marathas and five hundred Rajputs, who, true to the traditions of their splendid race, died at their posts. A few only, too desperately wounded to move, were found hiding and taken prisoners. It was a great achievement, but the death of his gallant comrade, who had stood by him in a hundred perils, was a sore grief to Shivaji. "I have won the den and lost the Lion," he said.

The war followed its normal course. The forts were re-taken, and Shivaji made his usual plundering expedition into the Konkan. Jinjera, as before, under its stout Abyssinian governor, proved too much for the invaders, but Surat was pillaged. The English factory, however, resisted the attack, and the Marathas withdrew on hearing of the approach of a Moghul force. Shivaji could now put into the field a force of forty thousand men, and in the following year he actually dared to risk an open engagement with a division of the Imperial Army. The result was completely successful; the Marathas, falling back, drew on the Mahommedans until they were in disorder, when their cavalry suddenly wheeled and delivered a smashing charge in the most brilliant style, literally cutting their opponents to pieces. The moral effect of the victory was enormous: the newly raised Maratha cavalry learned that they were a match for their opponents in the open field. Henceforth Moghul prestige was on the wane in the Deccan. The next two years were devoted to a successful campaign in Bijapur, again rent in two by faction; and finally, in 1674, Shivaji was crowned at Raigad as "Padshaha of the Hindus"—a title which he had nobly earned. The coronation was performed by a great saint from Benares, Gaga Bhat, on the 6th of June, and after it was over, the new King undertook the ancient ceremony of "weighing himself in gold," and distributing the sum among the poor. Among the spectators was Mr. Oxenham, the English agent from Bombay, who had come to negotiate a treaty with the Marathas. At the auspicious moment, salvoes of cannon were fired in all the forts, till from end to end of the Sahyadri range the birth of the Maratha Empire was proclaimed.

After his coronation, Shivaji appeared as the protector of the Deccan from the Moghuls. They, and not Bijapur, were his country's true foes. And so, after making an alliance with the King of Golconda, Shivaji had two grand objects in view. Firstly, he sought to enlarge his realm by a great invasion of the Carnatic, in the course of which he conquered Tanjore and Vellore; and secondly, he checked Moghul designs upon Bijapur, forcing the invaders back to Aurangabad. In the course of these operations, the great leader, worn out by years of toil, died of what appeared at first to be a trifling injury, on April 5th, 1680.

In appearance, Shivaji was a typical Maratha—short and wiry, with long arms and large feet, and the keen eye of the hillman. He was abstemious and frugal in his habits, and devoted to his mother, his children, and his country. Like many other great leaders, he believed himself to be under divine guidance; he took no step without the advice of his goddess Bhavani, and he was earnestly imbued with the sense of his mission to restore the independence of his people. His manner was frank, pleasing, and soldierly; he was adored by his men, and not a single case of rebellion or remissness occurred during his long absence in Delhi. Yet disobedience met with the sternest rebuke, and one officer elected to die in battle rather than incur his wrath. He demanded implicit obedience to all orders, and only his magnetic personality could have transformed a horde of freebooters into a disciplined army as he did. Though personally brave to a fault, he had the sense not to risk his life unnecessarily, knowing as he did that the cause would fall with his death. In his organizing ability, too, he showed the qualities which go to make a good general. It is the fashion of English writers to depict him as an assassin and a freebooter.[1] Freebooter he certainly was, for until his forces were fit to take the field, he could only hope to harass his enemy by sudden raids. Assassin he was not, according to the ethics of the day. Of the two murders attributed to him, that of the Raja of Javli was provoked by a dastardly attempt to entrap him, which had led to the deepest hatred between the two families; for there was little doubt that, had it succeeded, Shivaji would have ended his days, blinded or maimed, in the dungeons of the Adil Shahs. The death of

[1] On the other hand, Justice Ranadé's attempt to justify his hero at all costs is equally unfair. Shivaji was the product of his age, and not free from its faults by any means.

Afzul Khan was looked upon at the time as due to the man's own folly, and there is reasonable ground for believing that he met Shivaji for exactly the same purpose himself. The murder of the Comyn by Robert Bruce was far more unjustifiable, but it is never brought against him. Necessity knows no law; they were hard and cruel times, and Shivaji only did what his Mahommedan opponents never scrupled to do. Against these dark deeds we must place the fact that Shivaji never plundered shrines, even Mahommedan ones; he treated women and children with the utmost courtesy; he was chivalrous and merciful to conquered enemies, sparing the common soldier, and dismissing the officer with gifts. "He was a great captain," said Aurangzeb, his bitterest foe, when he heard of his death. "He persisted in rebellion, plundering caravans and troubling all men; but he was guiltless of the baser sins, and scrupulous of the honour of the Muslim women and children who fell into his hands."

VIII

THE ADVENTURES OF ROBERT KNOX.

VIII

THE ADVENTURES OF ROBERT KNOX.

1640-1720 A.D.

"The utmost Indian isle, Taprobane."—MILTON.

THE story of the invasion—for it amounts to nothing less—of India by the crowd of hungry adventurers who flocked to the East after Vasco de Gama doubled the Cape of Good Hope in 1498, forms a chapter of Indian history in itself. They were a motley crew—Spanish, Portuguese, Dutch, English,[1] French, and Italians—well-nigh as diverse as could be in their aims and character. The earliest visitors, stimulated by the evil example of the Spaniards in the New World, came principally to plunder. Then followed more permanent settlers, whose aim was to establish trading factories on the coast, and to set up permanent commercial relations between India and the West. Others, again, came on individual enterprises, attracted by love of adventure or in search of employment, to the Court of the Great Moghul, stories of which now began to reach Europe, and to make

[1] The first English vessel put into Surat harbour in August, 1608—a momentous day in the history of India.

people realize that the fabled "Wealth of Ormuz and of Ind" was not altogether a fable after all.

The accounts of what these visitors to the East saw and did are of singular interest to the student. The best descriptions of a nation are not seldom written by foreigners; for a man often passes over as not worth recording those details of every-day life in his own country which are precisely what the historian of the future regards with the greatest attention. How many of the speeches or battle-pieces of Thucydides, for instance, would we not sacrifice for a glimpse into a meeting of the Ecclesia when Cleon was "up," or into the theatre when an excited audience was watching, with critical attention, the latest drama of Euripides? This lends a peculiar charm to the reminiscences of Bernier, the garrulous jottings of Manucci, or the correspondence of the haughty Roe, bent upon maintaining the prestige of his country at any cost. They afford us an insight into the state of India which all the court journals and archives would never give us. The personage who forms the subject of this essay, however, differs in many ways from the ordinary type of adventurer in the East in the seventeenth century. Robert Knox, though he traded at the ports of Western India for many years, has nothing to tell us of the great Mahommedan Empire. His adventures were of a different kind. Driven by accident to shelter in a bay on the coast of Ceylon, he was carried off a prisoner to the heart of the island. There, for nearly twenty years, he lived in the little Buddhist kingdom of Kandy, among a people utterly uncontaminated by Western contact, keeping intact customs imported over two thousand years before from Northern India, which had long ago, with the extinction of Buddhism, disappeared from the land of their birth. Knox is a plain, unimaginative sailor; but his narrative, written in the nervous, homely prose which the Puritan, perhaps, owes so largely to his devotion to the English Bible, is a fascinating story of adventure, and remains, besides, one of the shrewdest and most accurate accounts of the Sinhalese which we possess.

The annals of Ceylon, preserved in that naive monkish chronicle, the *Mahavamsa*, have an interest all their own in the history of the East. From immemorial times the island had been visited by bands of invaders from the Indian coasts. The *Ramayana*, the Iliad of the Hindus, contains the earliest legend of these incursions; for Ravana, the Paris of the Indian epic, had carried off the lovely Sita, bringing upon himself and his city the vengeance which befell the luckless prince of Troy. But the first permanent settlement of the Aryans in Ceylon belongs to the sixth century B.C., when a prince named Vijaya, from Bengal, sailed with his followers from the harbour of Tamralipti[1] to found a new Salamis in the "Fair island of Lanka-dipa." It is, perhaps, not generally recognized that the colonizing spirit was almost as rife in ancient India as in Greece. Ceylon, Java, and Cambodia, still contain relics of the Hindu colonists who settled there. Indian ships found their way to the mouth of the Tigris and to the coast of Arabia, perhaps to East Africa. The modern embargo against crossing the "black water" is of recent origin, and probably dates from the reactionary Brahminism

[1] Tamluk.

which followed upon the decay and overthrow of the Buddhist creed.

The next great event in the history of Ceylon was its conversion to Buddhism by the emissaries of Asoka, about three centuries after the landing of Vijaya, and the subsequent history of the country deals chiefly with the deeds of the medieval Sinhalese kings, their fights against the Tamil invaders from the north, their piety and munificence, and the glories of the great city of Anuradhapura with its splendid shrines, its gigantic *dagabas*, and its two precious relics, the sacred Bodhi Tree and the Holy Tooth. But gradually, as time went on, the Sinhalese were driven out of Northern and Central Ceylon. Their great capital, or what was left of it by the plundering Tamils, fell into ruin; the few priests who remained at the shrines were unable to keep them in repair with the scanty alms they received; and the seat of the kingdom was transferred to Kandy, the little town which nestles in the lower ranges of the central mountain chain of the island. Here, protected by the impenetrable and malarious jungles which cover the foothills with a dense mass of vegetation, dwelt the Sinhalese kings, till their deposition by the British in 1815. In 1517 the Portuguese first gained a footing in the island, to be replaced, not quite a century later, by the Dutch, who built the great fortresses which still adorn the ports and other points of vantage on the coast; but these, as Knox says, touched only the fringe of the country, the heart of the island remaining practically unknown to the Western world.

Robert Knox was born in 1640. He came of an

old East Anglian family—the sturdy Puritan stock which manned the *Mayflower*, and provided Cromwell with his finest troopers. Knox, indeed, was a typical Puritan—hard and grim and surly, combining an unctuous, if sincere, piety of the psalm-singing order with a shrewd eye for business. Not over-scrupulous where money was to be made, he found it easy to reconcile the teachings of the Bible with a little African slave-trading. His redeeming feature was the dogged English pluck which brought him through his manifold perils unscathed. His father owned a merchant ship—the *Anne*, frigate, of 230 tons—in which he and his son had already made a successful voyage to Madras. In 1657 they set out again for the East. They visited the Persian Gulf, Surat, and Sumatra, and reached the Madras coast late in 1659, where, in the roads of Masulipatam, they met with a disaster. The *Anne* lost her mainmast in one of the storms which herald the approach of the north-east monsoon, and as there are no trees on the flat South Indian shore, there was nothing for it but to take her to the Ceylon coast. The great harbour of Trincomali afforded ample shelter in which the ship might be repaired; and the thick forests which cover the shore yielded all the timber necessary for the purpose.

Here, in the Kottiyar Bay, the *Anne* put in a few weeks later, and Knox and his father proceeded to open communication with the local Sinhalese officer. To their horror, one day, when they had landed and were awaiting the arrival of the natives under a large tamarind,[1] they were suddenly seized

[1] The tree still survives, and is marked by an (incorrect) inscription. It stands in the little Moorish village of Muttur, near the mouth of the Virugal River.

and secured. At the same time a boat's crew engaged in cutting timber was captured. The wily Sinhalese tried to tempt the ship to approach nearer the coast, and young Knox was sent to interview the mate for the purpose. He pluckily advised his ship-mates to do nothing of the sort; warning them of the plot, he ordered them to load their guns and to fire on any one who approached. The Sinhalese, seeing the impossibility of capturing the ship, desisted in their attempts, and after waiting as long as was prudent, those on board hoisted sail and made off. It must have been with heavy hearts that Knox and his father and their sixteen companions saw their last hope of liberty vanishing as the frigate made the entrance and disappeared round the woody heights of Trincomali, and their distress was augmented when they were placed, for safety, in separate villages, "Where we could have none to confer withal or look upon but the horrible black faces of our heathen enemies." And then began their long tramp to the mountain fastnesses of the Sinhalese. For days they marched "Through great woods, so that we walked as in an arbour, but desolate of inhabitants." Probably the party did not follow the main road running to Matalé, along which the mail coach now travels, but took a short cut through jungle paths known to themselves. The prisoners were treated with the utmost leniency and courtesy. They were fed upon the best produce of the country—rice and herbs and fruit—and allowed to travel at their own pace. Knox notes, with some humour, that "At every town where we came they used, both old and young, in great companies to stare at us; it was also great entertainment to them to observe our manner of eating without spoons, and that we could not take the rice up in our hands as they do, nor gaped and poured the water into our mouths out of pots according to the country's custom."

Arriving at the outskirts of Kandy, the prisoners were distributed in various villages, which were allotted for their maintenance. And so for months their weary captivity dragged on. They had nothing to do; for they had been captured to satisfy a caprice of the king, and were merely detained till he should tire of the pastime. They were not alone; shortly before thirteen men of the *Persia Merchant*, wrecked on the Maldives, had been brought to Kandy, and the town was crowded, besides, with Portuguese and Dutch deserters[1] and others, none of whom were allowed to return, or even to communicate with the outer world. A letter roused instant suspicion, and usually cost the bearer his life. For the King of Kandy, aware of the fate of the lowlanders, was determined to remain in complete isolation, and to have no dealings with the foreigners from the West, who, he knew, were easier to call in than to get rid of. At first the Englishmen, deceived by their good treatment, thought that they would quickly obtain their liberty; and when an old Portuguese priest warned them not to expect any such good luck, "They railed at him, calling him Popish dog and Jesuitical rogue. But afterwards, to their grief, they

[1] There were about sixty Dutchmen alone. Even ambassadors were not permitted to return alive. Eight wretched Frenchmen, envoys from a fleet which was cruising round Ceylon, were still prisoners when Knox escaped.

found it to be true as he told them." As time went on the elder Knox sickened and died, heartbroken at his hopeless lot, and racked with malaria. "Now in his old age, when his head was grown grey, to be a captive to the heathen, and to leave his bones in the eastern parts of the world, when it was his hope and intention, if God permitted him to finish this voyage, to spend and end the residue of his days at home with his children in his native country, and to settle me in the ship in his stead; these things did break his heart." And so he died, and Knox was left alone in the world. How he eked out his scanty resources by knitting caps, pedling, and gardening, is pathetically told in his autobiography. For reading he was reduced to great straits. His sole literature consisted of "*A Practice of Piety* and Mr. Rogers' seven treatises called *The Practice of Christianity*." "These," he says, "I had read so often over that I had them almost by heart. For my custom was after dinner to take a book and go into the fields and sit under a tree, reading and meditating, until evening; excepting the day when the ague came, for then I could scarce hold up my head." And so, "with none but the black boy (his negro servant, captured with the rest) and the ague for company," he passed sixteen weary months. The monotony, however, was greatly relieved by the happy purchase of a Bible, the sight of which rejoiced Knox's Puritan heart exceedingly. It was, indeed, little less than a miracle that an English Bible should have found its way to that distant spot. The old man who sold it to Knox said that he had picked it up when the Portuguese lost Colombo, among the loot of the town.

Knox was fishing when his boy brought him the news, and he tells us how he "flung away his angle," and, trembling with excitement, bartered the book for a cap which he had knitted.[1] "I hope the readers will excuse me," he adds, with a touch of real pathos, "That I hold them so long upon this single passage. For it did so affect me then that I cannot lightly pass over it, as often as I think of it, or have occasion to mention it."

Of the condition of the country and the habits of the people Knox has a great deal to say. The King, Raja Sinha II., was a capable monarch, spoilt, however, by the caprice and cruelty which is one of the predominating features of the character of the later Sinhalese kings. He ruled by terror; his very ministers were often put to death for a mere whim, and among his immediate entourage, none was safe for a day. Punishments of the most barbarous nature—impaling, trampling by elephants, and tortures of a horrible kind, were common. A rebellion which broke out in Knox's time failed, because the leaders were too frightened to press their attack home, when resolute action could not have failed to succeed; such was the awe which the monarch's personality inspired. The town of Kandy was guarded by parties of men who watched all the passes, and dense hedges of thorns, with narrow passages cut in them to admit only a man at a time, protected the roads. The King's army did not number more than thirty thousand men, but it sufficed to repel the

[1] Knox and his companions made a good deal of money by knitting and selling the "Red Tunis caps" worn by seamen of that day.

aggressions of the Dutch, and even to capture their outlying forts.

These wars were disastrous to Knox and his friends, who hoped to escape on one occasion when the invaders came close to the village where they were quartered. But the King quickly moved them into the hills, forcing Knox to abandon the garden and farm, with all the "Hogges and hennes" he had so laboriously reared. On the whole, however, the people were lightly and justly governed. They were prosperous and happy, and not over-taxed, and the tyranny of the King only affected those who came into immediate contact with him. The policy of *laissez-faire*, which distinguishes Oriental monarchies from our over-governed, over-systematized Western countries, left the people very much to themselves. Disputes were settled by the *panchayat*, which decides questions by the immemorial tradition of the district; crime was rare, and every man lived as he would, according to the customs of his caste. Of the central authority, except when called upon to take his share in some piece of "Royal Labour"[1]—to build a dam for a tank, a road, or a new palace for the King—he heard very little. Though every man's life lay at the mercy of the monarch, and men were sometimes executed without any apparent reason save the King's capricious fancy, this sort of tyranny affected the people at large very little. There was no need to toil; the land was fertile and well-watered, and sowing and reaping the rice-crops, with all those pleasant, beautiful ceremonies and merry-making, song and dance, which among simple peoples have grown up

[1] *Râjâ Kârya*, an old feudal custom in Ceylon.

around these seasons, was a joy rather than a task. For the rest, there were the religious festivals—the Perahara, with its elephants and painted devil-dancers, its fine shows and its merry-making; the bright moonlight nights, when the yellow-robed priests read *Bana* under the palm-trees, and expounded to their audience the stories of the births of the Lord Buddha, and what he did in the guise of a monkey, an elephant, a deer; the holy-days, when all the village, with cries of *Sâdhu*, went to lay flowers before the Bodhi Tree, or burn incense at the great white *Dâgaba* on the hill. A curious feudal custom prevailed on the Royal demesne. It was farmed out to certain individuals, who were bound to pay, either in kind or military service, in return for its tenure; but any one who chose might relinquish his lands if he found the conditions too hard for his liking. The little kingdom of Kandy, nestling in its mountain fastnesses, was, in its way, better governed than France, if not England, at the time.

Knox also gives us a good deal of curious information about the trade guilds and the crafts of the country. The craftsmen were under the protection of the provincial officers, or overseers appointed for the purpose. Some who were under Royal patronage lived on the King's manor, and rendered certain services in return for their land. Others held land on similar terms from the richly-endowed temples or religious orders, like the goldsmith, who was allowed half an acre in return for repairing the vessels used in the Perahara procession, or another who received a similar grant on condition that he re-gilt the sacred images in shrine every year, and supplied "A silver ring for the festival tree." It is especially to be remarked that "No artificers ever change their trade from generation to generation; but the son is the same as was his father, and the daughter marries only to those of the same craft. And her portion is such tools as are of use and do belong unto the trade; though the father may give over and above what he pleaseth."

Of the high social status of the smiths, their independence and pretensions, Knox gives a highly diverting account: "Next after the degree of Hondrews (nobles)[1] may be placed Goldsmiths, Blacksmiths, Carpenters, and Painters, who are all of one degree and quality. Heretofore they were accounted almost equal to the inferior sort of Hondrews, and they would eat in those artificers' houses, but afterwards they were degraded on this sort of occasion. It chanced some Hondrews came to a smith's shop to have their tools mended; when it came to be dinner time the smith leaves work and goes in to his house to dine, leaving the Hondrews in the shop; who had waited there a great while to have their work done. Now the smith, fearing lest their hunger might move them to be so impudent as to partake of his dinner, clapt to his door after him. Which was taken so heinously by those hungry people, that they all went and declared what an affront the smith had put upon them. Whereupon it was decreed that all people of that rank should be deprived of the honour of having the Hondrews to eat in their houses.[2] . . . These smiths, nevertheless, take much

[1] *Hâmaduru*, the Kandyan equivalent for the honorific *Mahât-maya* of the low-country.

[2] The story, no doubt, was invented to account for the actual status of the smiths. The point, however, is that the craft-guilds

upon them, especially those who are King's smiths, that is, such as live in the King's towns and do his work. They have this privilege, that each has a parcel of towns belonging to them, whom none but they are to work for. The ordinary work they do for them is mending their tools, for which every man pays to his smith a certain rate of corn in harvest time according to antient custom. But if any has work extraordinary, as making new tools or the like, beside the aforesaid rate of corn, he must pay him for it. In order to this they come in an humble manner to the smith with a present, bringing rice, hens, and other sorts of provisions, or a bottle of rack, desiring him to appoint his time when they shall come to have their work done. The smith sits very gravely upon his stool, his anvil before him, with his left hand towards the forge, and a little hammer in his right. They themselves who come with their work must blow the bellows, and when the iron is to be beaten with the great maul, he holds it, still sitting upon his stool, and they must hammer it themselves, he only with his little hammer knocking it into fashion. . . . That which makes these smiths so stately is because the townspeople are compelled to go to their own smith and none else. And if they should, that smith is liable to pay damages that should work for any in another smith's jurisdiction."[1] What a contrast this picture affords to the position of the craftsman of to-day!

held a position only inferior to the nobles. The craftsman was an honoured member of the community, an artist not a menial.

[1] See A. K. Coomaraswamy, *The Indian Craftsman* (London, 1909), *passim*. For similar conditions in Medieval England, see Carlyle's *Past and Present*.

The wise regulation which protected the guild-craftsman from undue competition, enabled him to enjoy the leisure which is essential to artistic production. Of the excellence of the workmanship of these craftsmen we may judge from Knox's description of the Royal Palace. "The Palace itself hath many large and stately gates two-leaved; these gates, with their posts, excellently carved; the iron-work thereunto belonging, such as bolts and locks, all rarely engraven. The windows inlaid with silver plates and ebony. On the top of the houses of his Palace and Treasury, stand earthen pots at each corner; which are for ornament; or, which is a newer fashion, something made of earth resembling flowers or branches. The contrivance of his palace is, I may say, like Woodstock Bower, with many turnings and windings and doors." He notes, however, that the exquisite stone-carving of the old temples of Anuradhapura and Polonnaruwa was now no longer executed, the art being practically a lost one. "The pagodas or temples of their gods are so many that I cannot number them. Many of them are of rare and exquisite work, built of hewn stone, engraven with images and figures; but by whom and when I could not attain to know, the inhabitants themselves being ignorant therein. But sure I am that they were built by far more ingenious artificers than the Chingulayes that are now on the land. For the Portuguese in their invasions have defaced some of them, which there is none found that hath skill enough to repair to this day." Of one beautiful ceremony in connection with the making of images, mention must be made.[1] "Some being devoutly disposed will make the image of this god (Buddha) at their own charge. For the making whereof they must bountifully reward the founder. But when the eyes are to be made, the artificer is to have a good gratification, besides the first agreed upon reward. The eyes being formed, it is thenceforward a god. And then, being brought with honour from the workman's shop, it is dedicated by solemnities and sacrifices, and carried with great state into the shrine or little house which is before built and prepared for it." It is a remarkable thing that Knox says nothing of the famous Palace of the Tooth, nor of the yet more famous relic it contains.

Of the habit of polyandry, which undoubtedly existed among the Kandyans, Knox says nothing, though he remarks severely upon the laxity of the marriage-laws of the country, which he stigmatizes, with Puritan bluntness, as "Little better than whoredom." The same freedom which characterized Kandyan life in other respects, was visible here too; women enjoyed a degree of liberty unknown on the Indian continent, and divorce was easily obtained by either party, being usually arranged by mutual consent. The light-heartedness and absence of restraint which characterized the people were also visible in their relations to the gods. It was not unusual, says Knox, for a man to abuse, mock, and maltreat the image of the luckless deity, and when the "Voice of the Devil" was heard, the phantom was usually abused roundly: "Beef-eating slave, begone, be damned, cut

[1] See Coomaraswamy, *op. cit.*, p. 75, for a more detailed account of the ritual of this ceremony.

his nose off, beat him a pieces!" are specimens of the choice epithets Knox heard used upon these occasions. Whereupon, "The Voice always ceaseth for a while, and seems to depart, being heard at a greater distance." Knox declared that he heard this "Devil's Voice" in the woods at night himself; it was shrill like the barking of a dog, and moved rapidly through the air. The dogs, he says, trembled and shook at the sound, and though it was never known to do any harm, "Either just before, or very suddenly after this voice, the King cuts off the people." Knox says the Voice was not heard outside the Kandy district; as a matter of fact, however, the lowlanders have a story of a peculiar whistling sound (probably due to a kind of lizard) which they attribute to an evil spirit. It is said to be dangerous, and is much dreaded by the villagers, who declare that it leaps upon the passer-by and strangles him. It is invulnerable except to a silver bullet—a potent weapon in all countries. Knox notices that demoniac possession, as in India, was not uncommon, the possessed person remaining "Speechless, shaking, quaking, and dancing, and will tread upon the fire and not be hurt; they will also talk idle, like distracted folk."

Knox had now been a prisoner for nearly fifteen years. His companions had mostly resigned themselves to their lot. The people were courteous and kind, food was plentiful, and many of them, supporting their actions, Puritan-fashion, with Scripture texts, had taken wives of the daughters of the land. To them, as to Tennyson's "Lotus Eaters":—

> "Most weary seemed the sea, weary the oar,
> Weary the wandering fields of barren foam,"

A DUTCH FORT ON THE CEYLON COAST.
(Photo by the Author.)

[*To face page* 163.

and they had no desire to return, even at the price of freedom, to the horrors of the seaman's life in the seventeenth century. But Knox had never relinquished his hopes of escape. He refused any thoughts of union with a native woman, and, at the risk of his life, even declined a tempting offer of employment at court. It began to be evident that the only way out of the King's dominions lay to the north, where the roads were carelessly guarded, the attention of every one being concentrated on the southern approaches, where the Dutch frontier forts provided a constant menace. Knox was now less vigilantly watched than before. The King had tired of him. He was well known among the people of the surrounding villages, where he and his companions, John Loveland and Stephen Rutland,[1] often went on protracted tours, pedling their goods. Gradually they extended these tours to the lowlands, working with infinite caution and deliberation, noting the roads and gathering the necessary information, and always pushing further and further ahead. Twice they were stopped. Once they had secured the services of Knox's former "black boy" as their guide, but Knox fell ill, and when he recovered, the boy was no longer forthcoming. On another occasion they were unable to proceed because owing to a drought it was impossible to cross the long tracts of jungle which lay on their route. The drought lasted for four years; the wells were all dry, and travelling was impracticable for man or beast.

[1] Loveland, Knox's best friend, died in October, 1760. Rutland, who escaped with Knox, again went to the East with him in 1681, but was dismissed for "following his old course of drinking," and died in Bengal. The "rack" of Ceylon was too much for him.

At last, however, the great opportunity came. It was September 22nd, 1679, when they set out, and slowly they descended to the plains. They passed Koswatte, where Knox's father lay buried. They hid in the jungle to avoid the Revenue Officers, then touring the district, and with much searching of heart they entered the examining post at Kaluwila, where dwelt a high official whose business it was to examine all the traffic passing along the great north road to the frontier. Putting on a bold face, however, they demanded to be admitted to the great man's presence, and explained that they had come to barter their wares for dried deer's flesh. To their infinite relief, he recommended them to try what they could do in the neighbouring villages, as deer, owing to the recent drought, were scarce. Overjoyed, they pushed on to Anuradhapura, doubly glad to get away, as messengers had just arrived from Kandy to warn the local officers to be on the look-out; for the King, in one of his suspicious moods, had just seized certain nobles and their families, and he was anxious that none of his victims should escape. But these, too, had no inkling of Knox's intentions; and he tells us how, the night before they left Kaluwila, he gave a farewell party, with dancers and tom-toms, which lasted nigh until dawn.

The next day they emerged from the jungle at Anuradhapurà, a vast grassy plain, surrounded by a sea of dense forest interspersed with great ruined *dâgabas* and the huge *wewas*, or lakes, constructed by the kings of the olden time. Here again they halted, gathering provisions for their final dash through the wilderness to liberty. Of the two Dutch towns which they might make for, Jaffna and Manaar, the latter was obviously the more accessible. It was impossible, however, to follow the great highway which joins the Jaffna road north of Anuradhapura, for there was a frontier post which no subject of the King of Kandy could hope to pass. And so they determined upon a bold course. They resolved to follow the Malwattu Oya, the stream which issues from the Anuradhapura lakes, knowing that it would at least take them to the coast. The first day of their travels, however, very nearly brought disaster, for they blundered suddenly upon the group of villages which borders on the Tissa Wewa lake, and were forced to hide in a hollow tree until nightfall. Then they crept out, and felt their way along the forest-paths. They still heard voices around them, for the land in the neighbourhood of the tanks is thickly populated, and the Sinhalese are a wakeful folk. But to the harassed fugitives they appeared like the sound of pursuers, and they were relieved when a herd of elephants, trumpeting and breaking the boughs, came between them and their supposed foes, for no native will venture into a jungle when elephants are about. "These elephants," says Knox, "were a very good guard behind us, and were, methought, like the darkness that came between Israel and the Egyptians. For the people, we knew, would not dare to go forward, hearing elephants before them." And so they cooked a scanty meal and snatched a few hours' sleep; but when the moon rose, they pushed on again. A new danger arose, not only from the animals—elephants, buffaloes, and panthers—driven by the great drought to the river, but from the wild men of the jungle, the Veddahs, whose rude huts they came across from time to time. Still they pushed on, passing, perhaps at the ancient Buddhist settlement of Tantri Malai, "A world of hewn stone pillars, standing upright, and other heaps of hewn stones, which I suppose formerly were buildings. And in three or four places are the ruins of bridges built of stone, some remains of them standing yet upon stone pillars. In many places are points built out into the river like wharfs, all of hewn stone; which I suppose have been built for kings to sit upon for pleasure." At last, their shoulders cruelly torn with the thorns, they emerged into the Tamil country, and here they found two Brahmins sitting under a tree. One of these, bribed with "five shillings, a red Tunis hat, and a knife," consented to guide them a little way, and once more they lay down under a tree to rest. Elephants were as plentiful as ever, and could only be driven away by flinging firebrands at them. And so, next day, they continued their weary march. The jungle now grew thinner and thinner, the soil flatter and more sandy. It was a sign, had they but known it, that the coast was not far off. Suddenly they saw a man; accosting him in broken Portuguese, they learnt that they were in Dutch territory. They were free! A few miles further they reached the little outpost of Arippu, and saw once more the surf breaking on the beach, and heard the sound of white men's voices. "We arrived," says Knox, "about four of the clock on Saturday afternoon, October 18th, MDCLXXIX. Which day God grant us grace we may never forget, when He was pleased to give us so great a deliverance from such a long captivity, of nineteen years, six months, and odd days, being taken prisoner when I was nineteen years old, and continuing in the mountains among the heathen till I attained to eight and thirty." A strange figure they must have made, wild and bearded, their shoulders cut and torn by the thorns, wearing nothing but tattered loin-cloths and mocassins of deer-skin. Next day they went to Manaar, where the Governor himself received them in his sumptuous house. "And it seemed not a little strange," Knox tells us, "Who had dwelt so long in straw cottages among black heathen, to sit on chairs and eat out of china dishes on a table." And so, after a long voyage—for passages to Europe were not easily to be had in those days, and Knox went from Manaar to Jaffna, Colombo, and finally Batavia—he arrived in sight of the white cliffs of England in September, 1680. What changes he must have found in the old country! The great Oliver dead, the Commonwealth long since at an end, and the Merry Monarch reigning once more on his father's throne!

One would have thought that Knox had now had enough of adventure. Far from it, however, he continued his voyages to the East for the next twenty years, nearly losing his life on one occasion at Madagascar. From time to time news came to him of his fellow-captives, some of whom escaped and found their way to the coast, the majority, however, dying in Ceylon. To them he addressed a letter, which, with other interesting papers, has lately been brought to light.[1] His consolatory remarks to these unhappy

[1] Found by the late Mr. Donald Fergusson in the Bodleian, and published by Mr. Ryan (Glasgow, 1911).

exiles are not without their comic side: "I have often mentioned your case to the English East India Company, but without effect, therefore I advise you to rely only upon God, Who worketh all things after the council of His own will, and consider the difficulty of aged persons to gitt a living as the two now in England doe find it. I find a man in his native country among his relations not free from troubles, many of which I was free from while on Zelone, in so much that I still continue a single man." Knox died in 1720, eighty years of age, and in no wise hurt by his strangely adventurous career. He is a typical example of those dour seamen whose dogged pluck built up our Eastern Empire. Obstinate and avaricious, he still commands our respect, if not our admiration, and his book is probably the most entertaining narrative of adventure in that adventurer's El Dorado, the East Indies of the seventeenth century, which has ever been written.

IX

RANJIT SINGH AND THE SIKH NATION.

IX

RANJIT SINGH AND THE SIKH NATION.

1780-1839.

To the north of the great Rajputana Desert lies the historic land of the Panjab, the country of the Five Rivers. Stretching from Delhi to Peshawar, it has, from time immemorial, stood at the gate of India. Countless invading hordes have rested in its rich fields on their way to the opulent Middle Country beyond. Here the Aryan tribes themselves found their first home, and here the Vedic Hymns were composed. Here Alexander built his great altars; and often, to this day, the ploughmen unearth coins of the Indo-Greek or Scythian monarchs who ruled in the land in distant ages, while ruined *stûpas* bear witness to the now-forgotten religion of the Buddha, long since, with its adherents, swallowed up in the dead past.

The race which we now know as the Sikhs is probably descended from various clans of the Jat or Scythian tribes which poured into India from beyond the Oxus in the first few centuries after Christ. Unlike their kinsmen, the gallant Rajputs, these quiet, rough farmers took little part in subsequent historical events. Ready enough to fight when molested, they possessed none of the picturesque chivalry of the knights of Rajputana. We do not hear of them as helping to repel the Mahommedan invasions, though doubtless many a Sikh fought under the banner of one or another of the Rajput chieftains. Like other Hindu peasants, they were quite oblivious of what went on in the great world beyond, so long as they themselves remained unaffected. It remained for a great religious revival to give them, as such revivals often have, a national consciousness.

In 1469, while the House of Lodi was maintaining a feeble and precarious hold upon the throne of Delhi, a boy named Nanak was born on the banks of the Ravi near Lahore. Religious movements were in the air. For the last three hundred years the Vaishnava revival had been exciting the fervour of the inhabitants of Southern India, and the movement gradually spread to the centre and north. It was the great Ramanand who first preached to the common people, and following the example of Gautama, gave them a religious literature in their own vernacular, instead of in the classical language of the Brahmins. Ramanand's disciple, Kabir, had a new problem to face. Opposed to him was the powerful and widespread creed of Islam. Was he to condemn it as false, to urge his followers to persecution and forcible conversion of the adherents of the rival sect? This, however, is not the attitude of Hinduism to opposing religions. Christianity and Islam, essentially missionary creeds, seek to stamp out and destroy their rivals; Hinduism takes the wider view. It holds that all religions are at heart one, and it seeks to embrace and include, rather than to extirpate. Herein lies the vitality of Hinduism. It has absorbed the creeds of the Dravidian of the south and the hill-man of the north, and it provides for the spiritual needs of the ascetic and the philosopher on the one hand, and of the simple peasant on the other. Such was the teaching of Kabir. "God is One," he said, "Whether we worship Him as Ali or as Rama. The Hindu worships God on the eleventh day, the Mahommedan fasts at Ramazan; but God made all the days and all the months. The Hindu God lives at Benares, the Mahommedan God at Mecca; but lo, He Who made the world lives not in a city made by hands.[1] There is One Father of Hindu and Mussalman, One God in all matter: He is the Lord of all the earth, my guardian and my priest." Kabir died in 1420, and his spirit stirred in young Nanak. He, too, determined to do for the people of the Land of Rivers what Kabir had done for the tribes of the Ganges valley, and so, putting away wife and child, he wandered to and fro preaching. Those who followed him he called *Sikhs* or Disciples, and the feeling of reverence for their first great teacher became the nucleus round which a powerful race grew up. He, like Kabir, believed in the exalted doctrine which found in Hinduism and Islam two expressions of the same truth. "There is no Hindu and no Mussalman," was one of the earliest of his sayings :—

[1] "The hour cometh when ye shall neither in this mountain, nor yet at Jerusalem, worship the Father. . . . The hour cometh, when the true worshippers shall worship the Father in Spirit and in Truth." (St. John iv. 21, 23.)

"Make Love thy mosque, Sincerity thy prayer-carpet, and Justice thy Quran;
Modesty thy circumcision, Courtesy thy Kaaba, Truth thy guru, Charity thy creed and prayer;
The will of God thy rosary, and God will preserve thine honour, O Nanak."[1]

Such was the song he uttered when the Mahommedan governor called upon him to explain this mysterious utterance. It is impossible to find words strong enough to reprobate the insane conduct of Aurangzeb in persecuting the followers of a saint who wished to unite Hindu and Mahommedan in a common creed. Had Akbar's wise policy been followed, such advances, reciprocated by the holders of *Sufi* doctrines on the other side, might have resulted in a united India, capable of resisting all comers, and producing a great literature and art in which the virtues of both races were reflected. Among his own countrymen, Nanak's efforts were devoted to preaching against caste, cruelty, and superstition. All are equal in the sight of God. It is not that which goes into the mouth, but that which comes out of the mouth, which defiles a man, he explained to those Brahmins who rebuked him for cooking and eating a deer caught by his disciples and presented to him. Equally striking were the verses he uttered on the subject of caste and ceremonial purification in his sermon to the assembled pilgrims bathing at Hardwar on the day of the great festival:—

Evil mindedness is the low-caste woman, cruelty is the butcher's wife, a slanderous heart the sweeper woman, wrath the pariah woman.

---

[1] Macauliffe, *Sikh Religion*, i. 38. Compare St. Paul's exhortations to "circumcise the heart."

What availeth it to have drawn lines round thy cooking-place, when these four sit ever with thee?

Make Truth, Self Restraint, and Good Acts thy lines, and the utterance of the Name thine ablutions.

Nanak, in the next world he is best who walketh not in the way of sin.[1]

Nanak wandered all over Hindustan, preaching alike in Jain temples, Brahmin shrines, and Mahommedan mosques the Oneness of God. By his side went Mardana, his faithful disciple, who played the lute while the Master sang his inspired lays. It is even said that on one occasion he performed the *Haj*, and it is told how, when he was reproached with sleeping "with his feet towards God" (*i.e.* with his feet towards Mecca), he replied, "Turn my feet in a direction in which God is not." It is also related that he met in his wanderings the Emperor Babar. A Moghul force had raided the village where the Guru was staying, and carried the Master and his disciple before their commander. Nanak preached his doctrine of the universal religion with his usual fearlessness before the court, and was honourably dismissed. In 1538 he died, and a pathetic legend is told of his end. He felt himself sinking, and bade his disciples sing the *Sohila*, the beautiful funeral hymn of the Sikhs:—

In the House where God's praise is sung, and He is meditated on, sing the Sohila and remember the Creator.

Sing the Sohila of my fearless Lord: I am a sacrifice to the song of joy by which everlasting comfort is obtained.

The year and the auspicious time for Marriage[2] are at hand meet me, my friends: anoint me with oil like a bride.

---

[1] Macauliffe, *Sikh Religion*, i. 52.

[2] Death is the mystic marriage of the soul with God. "The Spirit and the bride say, Come."

Pray, my friends, that I may meet my Lord. The message comes to every house: the invitation goeth forth every day.
Remember the voice of the Caller: *Nanak, the Dawn is at hand.*

The song had died away, and hearing his Hindu and Mahommedan followers contending whether he should be burnt or buried, he ordered them to spread a sheet over him, and said, "Let the Hindus heap up flowers on my right hand, and the Mahommedans on my left. Those whose flowers are fresh in the morning may have my body." In the morning both heaps of flowers were bright and fresh, and when they lifted the sheet, lo, there was nothing there.

Time went on, and the number of converts to the Sikh religion gradually increased. From being merely a religious sect, the "Disciples" began to assume the proportions of a nation. Unhampered by caste, and bound together by the ties of a common religion, they had, like Cromwell's Ironsides, a political as well as a religious reason for concerted action. A motive for combining together was soon found in the need for resistance to Mahommedan oppression. Under the liberal rule of Akbar the Sikhs had been tolerantly governed. Akbar's religious principles were Nanak's own, and there was little cause for discontent. But with the accession of Jahangir, provincial mismanagement awoke the latent antipathy of Hindu and Mahommedan, which never remains quiescent long in India. The restless Arjun, the fifth Guru, began his remarkable career about this time. He started building the Golden Temple at Amritsar, and in 1604 compiled the first edition of the *Adi Grantha*,[1] the Bible of the Sikh nation, containing the inspired

[1] *Grantha*, like *Bible*, means Book—*the* book, par excellence.

utterances of the Gurus. This venerable volume is still preserved at Khartarpur, and on holy days it is exposed to the gaze of the faithful. A copy was presented to Queen Victoria in 1861, and to-day Sikh regiments march with the sacred book at their head. In 1606 Arjun was put to death for joining in a rising against the Emperor. His sandal-wood staff at Khartarpur is still shown to pilgrims, in the handsome edifice built by Maharaja Ranjit Singh. The Sikhs continued to give trouble to their Mahommedan rulers under Hargovind, Arjun's son and successor; but the rebellion really flamed out under the disastrous rule of Aurangzeb, who usurped the throne in 1658. Aurangzeb set himself to stamp out infidels wherever he found them. Among the special objects of his animosity were the Sikhs. An Imperial Army ravaged the Panjab, and their Guru, Teg Bahadur, was dragged in chains to Delhi. "I see," he said dauntlessly to the Emperor, "A power rising in the West, which will sweep your Empire into the dust." His body was quartered and hung before the city gates; but the Sikhs never forgot his prophetic words. They have accounted largely for Sikh loyalty to British rule; and they were on the lips of the gallant Panjabi regiments before Delhi in 1857, when at last they avenged in blood the martyrdom of their leader. Teg Bahadur's son, Govind Singh, the last of the Gurus, fled to the hills when his father was taken. For years he studied and meditated, preparing for his future career, and at last one day he descended, with five disciples, into the plains, and announced his mission. Thousands flocked to his banner asking for baptism at his hands, and demanded to be led against the oppressor. Those who were thus enrolled were called the *Khalsa* or Elect;[1] they received the surname of Singh or Lion, and were soon ready to take the field against the Mahommedans, distracted as they were by the Maratha war. In the long war that followed, the saints enjoyed varying success. At first they were successful, and then again they were driven back. In one battle[2] the Guru's two eldest sons were killed; in another, the remaining two were captured and buried alive by the Governor of Sirhind. The Guru himself fled to the thick forests of Talwandi, where Nanak was born. Here he bode his time, to issue forth, when the moment seemed propitious, and reconquer most of what he had lost. On the town of Sirhind, where his children met their cruel doom, he laid a bitter curse, and to this day it is a heap of ruins. Guru Govind Singh fell by the assassin's dagger, in 1708. Aurangzeb had died the year before. His successor, Banda, carried on the campaign with vigour and success till 1716, when he suffered a disastrous defeat at the hands of the Moghuls. He himself was dragged off as a prisoner to Delhi, where he was paraded in an iron cage, wearing a crown and royal robes. Finally, he was made to kill his own child, and was then torn to pieces with red-hot pincers. His followers were remorselessly hunted down, and we hear no more of the Sikhs for many years. They were crushed, and well-nigh exterminated.

[1] They were enjoined to wear five distinctive articles of dress, the "five k's"—*kes*, *khanda*, *kanga*, *kâra*, *kuch*—long hair, dagger, comb, bangle, and breeches.

[2] Battle of Chamkaur, 1705.

About 1760, however, we find the Sikhs once more beginning to re-assert themselves. The Empire of Delhi, beset by the Marathas on the south, and the English on the east, was reduced by this time to a mere shadow. The policy of Aurangzeb had borne its bitter fruit. And then came the horror of fresh invasions from the north-west. First the Persians swooped down and carried off thirty millions of treasure from the doomed capital, with the peacock-throne of the Moghul Emperors; then horde after horde of Afghans burnt, plundered, and murdered from end to end of the country. The Sikhs, left to themselves, recovered much of their ancient prestige, and gave serious trouble to the Afghans. Time after time the Afghan general drove them back, but no sooner had he commenced to withdraw, than they pounced on the evacuated country, cut up outposts, and captured isolated forts and garrisons. The chief obstacle to their advance to a prominent position among the nations of India was their lack of unity. There was no central government. The land was split up among the twelve great feudal houses, and nothing could induce them to combine for concerted action. Each was intensely jealous of his neighbour, and intestine quarrels between the chiefs were not infrequent. During this time, the national character of the people had degenerated greatly. The exalted teaching of the Gurus was almost forgotten, and the Sikhs had become a race of robbers, whose only law was the sword. The castles of the feudal chiefs were the scenes of many a wild orgie. Drink, for all the prohibitions of the Grantha, was freely consumed; and the women, fierce, capable, and unbridled in their passions, were often the very antithesis of our conceptions of the Hindu wife and mother.

It was at this crisis in the history of the Sikhs that Ranjit Singh was born. His father, Mahan Singh, was the head of the Sukarchakia clan near Amritsar, and the boy was, almost from his birth, brought up in the field. At the age of ten, seated on his father's elephant, he took part in an attack on the Manchar fort and was within an ace of being killed. Two years later (1792) Mahan Singh died, and left the lad to rule as best he could as turbulent a mob of swordsmen as could well be imagined. For a time the young prince was in the hands of his mother-in-law, Sada Kour, head of the Kanhaya clan, and his mother, a dissolute but able woman, surrounded by many lovers who dictated the policy of her state. Ranjit Singh was not, however, the type of man to stand this sort of thing very long. Disgusted at his mother's amours, he is said to have killed her with his own hand, and his mother-in-law was locked up in a fortress. In 1799 Ranjit Singh scored his first diplomatic success. Shah Zeman, Amir of Afghanistan, had occupied a great part of the Panjab, including the capital town of Lahore. In that year, however, he was recalled by a sudden outbreak to Afghanistan, and left so hastily that he was forced to abandon part of his artillery. Guns in those days were supremely valuable, and Ranjit Singh volunteered to forward them to Kabul if he were allowed in return to occupy Lahore. The Afghan monarch gladly consented, and Ranjit Singh marched in and took possession, to the wild jealousy of the neighbouring chiefs. In 1802 he followed up this success by driving the Bangi chiefs out of Amritsar, and seizing the city. Amritsar, with its Golden Temple and the great *Zam Zam*[1] gun, was second only in importance to Lahore in the eyes of the Sikhs. By 1807 Ranjit Singh had acquired a kingdom in the Panjab such as few would have dared to dream of, considering the fierce and turbulent elements of which it was composed. The Lahore, Amritsar, and Jalandhar districts had submitted; the Kanhaya tribe, headed by his mother-in-law, held out for some time, and even tried to call in the English; but the stout old lady was captured and her property confiscated. The rest of the confederacy was paralyzed at the Maharaja's swiftness. "These Kanhayas were always cowardly dogs," said Ranjit Singh in open durbar. Stung by the taunt, Jodh Singh defied Ranjit Singh in his fort for many weeks, while another stronghold under a slave girl made an equally gallant stand. But resistance was useless, and Maharaja Ranjit Singh soon found himself master of practically all the Sikhs east of the Sutlej.

The great aim of the Maharaja was to unite all the Sikhs under his sceptre, and he was determined, about 1806, to cross the Sutlej and conquer the Phulkian rajas, whose rapacity and misrule had reduced the country to a state of abject misery.

[1] This famous gun now stands outside Lahore Museum, and has been immortalized by Kipling in *Kim*. Cast by Ahmad Shah in 1768 out of water-pots collected as *jaziah* from the Hindus, it was seized by the Bangis, carried off by Charat Singh, captured by the Mahommedans and taken to Ahmednagar, seized once more by the Bangis, and finally captured by Ranjit Singh, who used it in all his campaigns. For its romantic story, see Griffin and Massey's *Panjab Chiefs* (1909), i. 479, *note*.

Here, however, he came in conflict with the English. The English policy had been to hold all the country up to the Sutlej. From the Sutlej to the Khyber they were willing, even desirous, to see Ranjit Singh's power fully established, for he would then be a valuable ally and form a convenient buffer against invasions on the part of the Afghans and possibly of the Russians or French. Further than the Sutlej, however, Ranjit Singh could not go without encroaching upon English rights: the great river formed a convenient and natural boundary. At first the Maharaja was bitterly incensed. He even thought of war, but fortunately the wise counsels of his great and learned Minister Aziz-u-din prevailed. Ranjit Singh saw that the moment he crossed the river, his numerous enemies in the Panjab would rise and throw off his yoke. The Afghans would swoop down upon his country from the north, and he would meet the fate of the Marathas and other races who had been rash enough to try conclusions with the British. One thing, too, he realized. No untrained troops, however brave, could hope to stand up against disciplined forces trained on Western lines. This had been the secret of English success in India; and Ranjit Singh saw that, if he wished to be anything more than a mere barbaric chieftain, he must organize his regiments. It was for this reason that he called in two distinguished officers of Napoleon's army, Ventura and Allard, to train his forces; while four other Europeans, Court, Gardner, Van Courtlandt and Avitabile, occupied positions of trust in the state. At the same time he made a treaty with the English, engaging not to cross the Sutlej, and determined to give his attention in the future to conquests in the south-east and north-east of the Panjab.

And so Ranjit Singh spent the rest of his career in campaigns against his Indian and Afghan neighbours. The first object of his attack was the Mahommedan fortress of Multan. He was repulsed in his first attempt in 1810, and skirmishing went on in an irregular fashion till January, 1818, when the Maharaja determined to make a final effort to reduce the town. Multan was invested, and the great Zam Zam hurled her huge stone balls against the ramparts, but all in vain.[1] Behind the outer walls arose a second wall, and storming parties failed to surmount them. Time went on, and by June only about two hundred of the garrison were left alive. Even then no one suspected the state of the defenders till a party of Akalis, a fanatical clan, suddenly made a rush on one of the bastions and captured it. It was then seen that the town was practically deserted, and the Sikhs soon drove in the little garrison. The slaughter went on, and at last only the old Commandant, Muzaffar Khan, and his eight sons were left. They stood with their backs to the wall, cutting down all who approached within reach of their swords, till at last the Sikhs fell back and picked them off one by one with their muskets. And so Multan fell, and the Maharaja returned to Lahore with two crores of rupees' worth of plunder. Another undertaking which had occupied much of the Maharaja's attention

[1] It is recorded that the great gun was fired no less than *four times!* Baber records with exultation in his memoirs that one of his howitzers, at the battle of Agra, got off six shots in the day.

about this time was the conquest of Cashmere. In 1811 he formed an alliance with the Afghans of Kabul to attack the country, but the heavy Sikh troops, unused to mountain fighting, and hampered by the snow, did little good, and the Afghans refused them a share of the spoils. In revenge Ranjit Singh, by a trick, induced the commander of the important fort of Attock, which guards the chief ford over the Indus from the Khyber Pass, to admit his troops. The Afghans who came to try and recapture the place were defeated in a pitched battle. For the first time in history the Sikhs had worsted their old rivals in the open field, and Ranjit Singh began to reap the reward of his careful reorganization of his forces. Cashmere was finally annexed in 1819, the year after the fall of Multan, and added considerable territory, if not very much actual increase of income, to the Maharaja's possessions. One by one the chieftains of the Panjab were reduced, and then Ranjit Singh determined to round off his conquests by the reduction of Peshawar. The Maharaja was now beginning to feel the effects of a career of incessant activity, only relieved by fierce drinking bouts in his occasional intervals of leisure. In 1825 he was so seriously ill that two chiefs actually plotted to seize the Amritsar fort, so as to have a claim on the district in the event of the Maharaja's death. The English physician who was called in warned Ranjit Singh that unless he gave up drinking, the results would be serious. The old warrior recovered, however, and spent the next ten years in a series of not very profitable campaigns in the Peshawar district. The Sikhs could really make very little headway against the wild Pathan tribesmen, though Peshawar itself was taken in 1835, by one of those *ruses* at which Ranjit Singh was so proficient.

Shortly before this, negotiations had been opened between Ranjit Singh and the English, in view of the ominous advance of the Russians through Eastern Persia towards the borders of Afghanistan. Ranjit Singh never loved the English, and viewed them with suspicion and distrust.[1] The great majority of his subjects cordially shared his feelings, and it was only the Maharaja's prudence which restrained them from breaking the peace. As early as 1809 the British envoy at Lahore had been attacked by an infuriated mob, and it is said that the steadiness of his small bodyguard first impressed Ranjit Singh with the value of discipline, and made him recognize the futility of a war with a nation who had thousands of such men at its back. In this case, however, concerted action was obviously advisable. If Herat fell, Afghanistan would be in danger. Already, in Lord Amherst's time, a friendly exchange of presents between the Maharaja and the Viceroy had taken place, and at the end of the rainy season of 1831, a grand durbar was held at Rupar on the Sutlej, where the two great potentates met in state. This eastern Field of the Cloth of Gold must have presented a superb spectacle. The flower of the Sikh chivalry were there—heads of houses older than the days of Alexander—with their shining armour and

[1] A story is told of how a youth who had been educated in British India was showing the Maharaja a map. "What are those red circles?" asked Ranjit Singh. On being told that they represented British spheres of influence, "Curse them," he is said to have exclaimed, "It will be all red soon."

heron plumes in their helmets. Less brilliant as a spectacle than these wild cavaliers, but more reliable for the purposes of modern warfare, were the trained regiments of sepoy infantry, organized by General Ventura, and the special object of the Maharaja's solicitude. For days the troops and their leaders fraternized, and in the sports and tourneys Ranjit Singh, in spite of advancing years and incipient paralysis, displayed his superb horsemanship to the admiration of all. The diplomatic object of the Viceroy was to arrange with the Maharaja some plan by which the safety of Afghanistan could be secured; for there was a grave risk that the Amir might seek safety in a voluntary alliance with Russia and Persia. In that case, it would be only a question of time before a combined Russian, Persian, and Afghan army appeared in the Khyber Pass. The final result of this interview was the fatal policy of placing Shah Shuja on the throne under the protection of British troops—a course of action which resulted in utter disaster and humiliation. Shah Shuja was quite unsuited to rule the turbulent tribesmen of Afghanistan. They detested and despised him. For years he had been an exile in the Panjab, and his attempt to regain the sceptre in 1831 ended in an ignominious failure. His brother, the gallant Dost Mahommed, the hero of the famous battle against the Sikhs outside Attock, was, on the other hand, universally popular. But Dost Mahommed refused to listen to the British envoy unless he promised to procure the restoration of Peshawar to Afghanistan, and this the English could not do without betraying Ranjit Singh. Hence it seemed best to the Government to depose Dost

Mahommed and place upon the throne one who would be more subservient to their wishes. Ranjit Singh looked upon Shah Shuja with the utmost contempt. A story is told of how, when he first came as a fugitive to Lahore with the famous Koh-i-nor in his possession, the Maharaja bullied, threatened, and finally starved him, in order to wring the jewel from the poor exile.[1] To have a monarch of this kind on the throne of Afghanistan meant revolution and disorder, which would suit Ranjit Singh admirably. For this reason he promised such co-operation as he could give to the British invasion of Kabul, only stipulating that the expedition should march through Sind, and not through his territory. It was when the expedition had just arrived at Kandahar that Ranjit Singh died, on June 27th, 1839, not quite sixty years old. He had been paralyzed for some time, and hard drinking hastened the end.

So died the last of the great independent chiefs of Hindustan. He had few of the milder virtues; a heavy drinker, dissolute in morals, unscrupulous where an end was to be gained, he nevertheless commands our unstinted admiration. He started life as a petty chieftain ruling a few miles of barren territory and commanding a few hundred irregular horse. In less than half a century he had subdued the whole of the Panjab, conquered Cashmere, and organized a well-trained force of 30,000 disciplined troops. A contemporary traveller describes him as a little man, with long arms and a countenance pitted with small-pox. He had a wrinkled face and a scanty grey beard. Only on horseback, with his small

[1] Griffin, *Ranjit Singh* (Rulers of India), 1911, p. 101.

black shield over his shoulder and his troops behind him, did he appear the man he was. His skill and courage as a horseman were extraordinary, in spite of the fact that he was crippled by paralysis. He had an overmastering passion for horses, and there is a well-known story of how he waged a long and deadly war with Yar Mahommed of Peshawar, in order to force him to surrender the grey mare Laili, the loveliest horse in Asia. She cost him "sixty lakhs and twelve thousand good men"; and she lived in a palatial stall with golden bangles round her legs. Ranjit Singh was careless about his personal appearance. He was usually dressed in a plain suit of khaki, without jewels. But his tremendous personality overawed all who came near him. He had early in life lost one eye with small-pox. His minister was once asked which eye it was. "The splendour of his face is such," replied Aziz-u-din, "That I have never dared to looked close enough to discover."

With the subsequent history of the Sikh race we are not now concerned. After the death of their grim ruler, no one could restrain them. English prestige had suffered severely from the Afghan fiasco of 1842, and in 1845 the Khalsa madly determined on war. There could only be one end to the struggle; yet in the two campaigns of 1845 and 1846, thanks to the careful training of their late ruler, the Sikhs faced a large and fully equipped British army in the open field, and on one occasion came very near to winning a victory. The Sikh campaigns were undoubtedly the sternest and hardest in the history of British India. Like the gallant nation they are, the Sikhs bore us no ill-will for a fair beating in open battle; eight years after the flower of their chivalry had fallen at Gujarat, they took the field against the mutineers at Delhi, when all India seemed to be pitted against us.

X

FOREIGN INFLUENCES IN THE CIVILIZATION OF ANCIENT INDIA.

X

FOREIGN INFLUENCES IN THE CIVILIZATION OF ANCIENT INDIA.

"Dan, also, and Javan going to and fro occupied in thy fairs; bright iron, cassia, and calamus, were in thy market."—EZEKIEL xxvii. 19.

I

TRADE between India and the West, both by land and sea, stretches, no doubt, beyond the dawn of history. But for a long time it was fitful and intermittent. By land the journey was beset with perils, deserts, mountains,[1] and hostile tribes. By sea, navigation was hindered by bad ships and want of enterprise on the part of the sailors. It was not until the Phœnicians, the greatest maritime nation, perhaps, in all history, undertook the task of exploring Eastern waters, that anything serious was achieved in this direction. Curiously enough, this important step was not due to any of the powerful nations of Asia Minor, the Egyptians, or Assyrians, but to the enterprising action of Solomon, the ruler of the tiny Hebrew Kingdom of Israel, some time in the twelfth century B.C. Solomon, upon coming to the throne, found his country in a state of almost unexampled prosperity, and determined to make Jerusalem as

[1] Ibn Batuta, the Moor, who did the journey in the thirteenth century, said that the Hindu Kush Mountains (*i.e.* Hindu-slaying Mountains) were so called because so few Hindu captives survived the journey over them.

magnificent as the capitals of his great neighbours. Unable, however, to obtain in sufficient quantities locally the gold, silver, and rare woods required for his purpose, he requested his ally, Hiram of Tyre, to lend him some of his skilled seamen to build a fleet for use in Eastern waters. Making their headquarters the port of Ezion-Geber, the modern Akaba, at the northern extremity of the right arm of the Red Sea, these sailors fitted out a number of vessels, in which with characteristic boldness they soon passed the Straits of Bab-el-Mandeb. Their final destination was the port of Ophir, from which they brought back as much as "four hundred and twenty talents of gold," as well as almug-wood, ivory, apes, and peacocks. The voyage to Ophir and back occupied a space of three years.[1]

There are many reasons for thinking that the port of Ophir was somewhere on the Indian coast.[2] The mention of the vast quantities of gold exported from it, seems to favour an identification of it with the "Barbarikon" of the Greek traders, which stood at the mouth of the Indus. The Indus valley, in ancient days, produced an enormous amount of gold; it paid Darius three hundred and sixty talents weight of gold-dust yearly in tribute;[3] and every one in Greece had heard of the legends of the miners of Dardistan and their fierce yellow mastiffs, which travellers in some extraordinary fashion mistook for

[1] See 1 Kings ix. 26 and 2 Chron. ix. 21.

[2] Perhaps, however, it was at the mouth of the Persian Gulf, and was an entrepôt visited by Indian traders, where they bartered their goods with the Phœnicians.

[3] Herod. iii. 97. A huge sum, equal to 4680 talents in Eubœic money; about £1,300,000 sterling. The mines were quickly exhausted, but gold is still extracted in small quantities.

huge ants! Again, the fleet of Solomon took three years to sail from Ezion-Geber and back. The voyage, then, took about eighteen months, and this was exactly the length of the voyage of Scylax of Caryanda from the Indus to the Gulf of Suez.[1] Ivory, apes, and peacocks would naturally come from an Indian port; and the Hebrew word for "ape," *koph*, is suspiciously like the Sanskrit *kapi*.[2] The "peacock," on the other hand, appears to have reached the West from a Dravidian port, perhaps Mangalore, the Roman Muziris, for the Hebrew word for a peacock, *thuki*, is, apparently, derived from the Tamil *tokei*, whence also the Persian *tavus* and the Greek Ταϝῶς. Many other commodities appear to have been introduced by these traders and their successors, to judge by their names. Thus the Greek σάνταλον (sandal, perhaps the "almug" of Solomon) is the Sanskrit *chandana*;[3] σινδών, linen, may be derived from the "Sindhu," or Indian country,[4] and may have been brought by Hebrew traders to the West; for we find *Sadîn*[5] used as "fine linen" in Isaiah, and *Sâtin* is the Arabic for a "covering." The word is also found in Assyrian. In a similar fashion, rice was brought to Europe by Arabian traders from Dravidian ports,

[1] Herod. iv. 44.

[2] Egyptian *kafu*. The Hebrew *shen-habbin* (elephant's teeth) is the Skt. *ibha-danta*, Egyptian *ebu*, Latin *ebur*. The Greek ἔλεφας is the same word with the Arabic *el* prefixed. ἔλεφας and κασσίτερος (Skt. *kastîra*) are both found in Homer, which points to an early (indirect) trade between Greece and India.

[3] For *ch* = Σ, *cf*. Chandragupta, Sandracottus.

[4] Like *Calico* (Calicut), *Muslin* (Mosul), etc.

[5] Isaiah iii. 23. See Sayce, Hibbert Lectures, 1887, p. 138. So, too, *cotton* is *karpasa* in Sanskrit, *karpas* in Hebrew, and κάρπασος in Greek.

for the word *rice* is a shortened form of the Spanish *arroz*, derived from the Arabic *aruz*, from which, too, the Greek ὄρυζα and the Latin *oryza* also come; and the Arabic word is simply a corruption of the Tamil *arisi*. The rich fields of Southern India must have borne rice-crops for immemorial ages.[1]

But the strangest and most interesting evidence of intercourse between India and Judæa in the time of Solomon is afforded to us by a Buddhist birth-story called the *Mahôsada Jâtaka*.[2] Here we have the story of a Yakshini, or female ghoul, who has carried off a poor woman's child in order to devour it. The mother claims her offspring, and the two women are summoned to the judgment hall of the Buddha (at that time incarnate as the wazir of the Rajah of Benares), to have their dispute adjudicated. The Buddha tells one woman to take the child's legs and

[1] Another plant known to Europe by its Tamil name was the *jack fruit* (Latin *pala*, Tamil *pala*). The dictionaries translate *pala* as "plantain," but Pliny's description of the tree is conclusive. "Fructum cortice emittit, longitudine trium cubitorum." (*N. H.* 12. 6.) Fancy a plantain three cubits long growing out of the bark of a tree! Dr. Caldwell, in his *Dravidian Grammar*, has made a list of the Tamil words thus taken by traders to the West. Hebrew *ahal*, "aloes," Tamil *ayhil*; κάρπιον, "cinnamon" (Ctesias), Tamil *karppu*; ζιγγίβερις, *inchiver* (ginger), etc. Spices have always been a favourite export from the East, perhaps, till tea, coffee, and rubber took their place, the principal one. The Dutch made a fortune out of *cinnamon*. *Pepper* was, curiously enough, consumed in huge quantities in Rome. Alaric demanded as part of his ransom 3000 lbs. of pepper. (Mukerji, *Indian Shipping*, p. 127.) The Zamorin of Calicut wrote to the King of Portugal, when Vasco de Gama visited him, "In my kingdom there is an abundance of cinnamon, cloves, ginger and pepper." Most of these came from the Dravidian ports.

[2] Rhys Davids, *Buddhist Birth Stories*, p. xiv. Cowell and Rouse's translation, vi. 163 (Cambridge, 1907).

the other its head, and decide the matter by a tug-of-war. The Yakshini consents, but the rightful mother will give up all her claims rather than put the baby to such torture. The Buddha then gives her the child. No one, I think, can doubt that this is an Indian version of the famous story of the Judgment of Solomon,[1] nor will anybody who has studied the extraordinary history of the migration of the Jâtaka Tales, be surprised at this odd occurrence. There can be no doubt that the Indians borrowed the tale from the Jews, and not *vice versâ*. The Jâtakas were collected from all sorts of præ-Buddhistic folk-legends. The only question is whether the Indians got it direct from Hebrew traders long before the birth of Gautama, or whether it came from Babylon, whither it had been brought by the Jews during the Captivity (597–538 B.C.).[2]

After the death of Solomon, the Persian Gulf became the chief trade route between India and Asia Minor.[3] At the mouth of the Euphrates lived the Chaldeans, a restless, seafaring race; the prophet Isaiah speaks of the "Chaldeans whose cry is in their ships,"—a vivid phrase, describing exactly the bustlo and turmoil of an Oriental port. About 695 B.C., however, Sennacherib, King of Assyria, replaced them by Phœnicians, probably in order to punish the

[1] 1 Kings iii. 16.

[2] During Gautama's lifetime. See, too, the story of the merchants who took crows and peacocks to Babylon. (*Baveru Jâtaka*, Cowell and Rouse, iii. 83.)

[3] For the facts about the Phœnicians and Babylonians, I am indebted to Mr. Kennedy's article on *Early Commerce of India with Babylon*: *J.R.A.S.*, 1898, and Professor Mukerji's *Indian Shipping*.

Chaldeans for helping the Babylonians in a rising against the Assyrian Empire. The advent of the Phœnicians had the same magical effect upon the trade of the Persian Gulf as it had formerly produced in the Red Sea. These bold navigators soon pushed on to India, and rounding the Indian coast, even visited the Malay Archipelago and China. A whole colony of Phœnician sailors sprang up in the Persian Gulf. The Bahrein Islands were especially popular as a port of call for vessels to take in water and provisions before setting out on their long run across the Indian Ocean, and recent excavations have revealed remains of a large settlement there.[1] Strabo says that in his day the islands of the Persian Gulf were dotted with Phœnician temples.[2] Their less skilful rivals, the Chaldeans, discontented at their supersession, appear to have rebelled again. This time they were banished to Gerrha, a terribly hot, barren spot, where they had to use blocks of salt to build their houses.[3] This must have been an unwelcome change after the humid climate of Chaldea.

Of the overland route between India and the West we hear little before the time of Darius the Great, probably because the journey was rendered difficult and dangerous by the wild tribes who beset the road. Even in the remotest days, however, such a route must have existed; an axehead of white Chinese jade

[1] The last Report of the Archæological Department gives details of these. Some of the remains have been put in the Prince of Wales's Museum, Bombay.

[2] *Geog*. xvi. 3. 3–5.

[3] Strabo, *Geog*. xiv. 33. This is not a traveller's tale. Ibn Batuta, the Moorish traveller, tells the same story about the negroes in the Sudan.

was found in the second city of Troy.[1] Caravans came and went, no doubt, both from Tyre and from the ports further north. In any case the route taken must have been ultimately the same,—past the Caspian Gates, and north of the Carmanian Desert to Balkh, where the roads running to China and India converged. S̱halmaneser (858 B.C.) has representations of Indian elephants and apes[2] and Bactrian camels on his obelisk, and these animals, the elephants at any rate, must have been imported overland. After the defeat of Assyria by Nebuchadnezzar in 606 B.C., Babylon became the leading city of Asia. In its market-places met the nations of the world,—captive Jews, Indian traders, Egyptian ambassadors, Phœnician sailors from the Far East—in short, as Berosus says, πολὺ πλῆθος ἀνθρώπων ἀλλοεθνῶν, "a crowd of men of all nationalities." We hear in one of the Jataka Stories of the adventures of the merchants who took the first peacock to Babylon; on the other hand, there appears to have been a settlement of Babylonian traders at the frontier town of Taxila in India, for Aristobulus of Cassandria[3] found at that city a "marriage-market" being carried on Babylonian fashion, just as is described by Herodotus.[4] What was the result of the contact been India and the Semitic races? Not very great, I think. Casual traders do little towards the real opening up of a country. From the Jews India learnt practically nothing; from the Chaldeans she may have borrowed

[1] The "Swastika" sign has, I believe, been found in Troy.

[2] For methods of trapping apes (apparently for export), see Aelian, *apud* McCrindle, p. 149.

[3] *Apud* Strabo, *Geog.* xv. 62–1.

[4] I. 196.

part of her præ-Alexandrian system of Astronomy;[1] from the Babylonian merchants may have come the idea of striking rude, punch-marked coins, and perhaps a system of weights and measures. It is, I think, useless to attempt to trace early Indian architecture to Babylonian or Assyrian sources. "The culture of Assyria, and still more of Babylonia, was essentially literary; we miss in it the artistic spirit of Egypt or Greece. In Babylonia the abundance of clay and want of stone led to the employment of brick; the Babylonian temples are massive but shapeless structures of crude brick, supported by buttresses."[2] The absurd stories of Ctesias about an Assyrian invasion of India, narrated by Justin,[3] are a gross fabrication, and Semiramis is a product of the imagination. The Semites merely prepared the way for the momentous Iranian invasion, with which we shall presently deal.

While thrones were rising and falling in Western Asia, a revolution of another kind was taking place in North-Eastern India. Gautama Buddha (568–488 B.C.)[4] was formulating the doctrines which were destined, to use the picturesque phrase of the Pali commentator, to re-echo "like a great bell set in the heavens" throughout the East. Gautama Buddha

[1] It has been also suggested that the story of the Tortoise Incarnation of Vishnu is a Hindu version of the story of the Flood, which first appears in Babylonian legend. Dr. Vogel attributes to Babylon the practice, in India and modern Europe, of naming the days of the week after the Sun, Moon, and five planets. This is a very interesting explanation of a remarkable coincidence.

[2] *Encyc. Brit.*, XIth Edn., "Babylonian Art."

[3] Justin, i. 1–3, etc.

[4] Dr. Fleet's date.

is the one personality of the præ-Alexandrian period of whom we can really say that we *know* something. Was he really an Aryan, or are we to class his remarkable crēed among the "foreign influences" which affected India during this period? The question is a startling one, and has never, I think, been adequately considered. But every one must have noticed the many striking features of Buddhism, so utterly at variance with anything to be found elsewhere in Hinduism, the *stûpa*, the worship of relics, the abolition of caste as a religious factor, contempt for penance and ceremonies, and the discouragement of abstract metaphysics. Many of these peculiarities may, of course, be merely the products of a powerful and far-reaching mind, bent on religious reform; but relic-worship, and its concomitant the *stûpa*, are quite un-Indian.[1] Gautama belonged to the Sakya clan: were they an early offshoot of the Sakas, the Sacæ or Scyths, who, as we know, followed the Aryans from time to time into India in successive waves? The word *stûpa* signifies a "barrow," or "tumulus," a Sanskrit name for a Scythian object. The Scythian chieftain was buried under a tumulus of this kind, and not, as in India, cremated. Herodotus, for instance, tells us how the Gerrhi, a tribe on the Borysthenes, buried their kings in huge square tombs, over which the people raised a high mound of earth, each vying with his neighbour to make it as tall as possible.[2] In Southern Siberia may be seen to this day the *kurgans* of the primitive Scythian tribes. The round shape of the *stûpa* shows that it was originally

[1] The Babylonians, of course, practised urn-burial.

[2] Herod. iv. 71.

an earthen structure,[1] just as the pyramid, a kindred type of building, must have been always constructed of stone. And so the massive Sanchi Stupa, with its elaborately carved stone railing, is very probably the lineal descendant of the rude earthen mound covering the tombs of the Scythian chieftains on the Central Asian steppes, fenced in by a rough palisade of huge logs, decorated with fetish-symbols to scare away the evil spirits which might otherwise disturb the peace of the inmate.

When the Saka tribes migrated to India, and were received into the fold of Hinduism, a kind of compromise must have been effected, in the case of notable personages, between the rival customs of burial beneath a barrow and cremation. The body was first cremated and then the ashes were buried. The custom of relic-worship—not a Hindu custom [2]—led to the practice of dividing the ashes (and other remains) of a deceased teacher among several claimants, each of whom enshrined his portion under a *stûpa* of his own. Thus the *stûpa*, or burial mound, became a *dâgoba*, or relic-holder. The earliest record of such a division relates to the ashes of Gautama Buddha himself.[3] Eight tribes sent delegates to claim, on the ground of kindred with the deceased teacher, a share of his remains.

[1] Fergusson thinks it was copied from the conical Tartar tents. But it is difficult to account for such an imitation. And the early stûpas are more dome-shaped. Professor Rapson (Hastings' *Dictionary of Religion*) traces it to the funeral pyre. But the resemblance is not very close.

[2] Perhaps a survival of the old barbarous rites paid to the "Manes" of deceased ancestors by various nations, particularly Mongolian nations. If the Scythians were-Mongolian in origin, we have another interesting piece of evidence in this custom.

[3] *Mahâparanibbana Sutta.* S.B.E., xi. p. 131.

The possession of such relics was, of course, an asset of great material value; the dagaba beneath which they lay became a *tîrtha*, or place of pilgrimage, and rapidly grew rich and famous.

Among the tribes claiming, as kinsmen, a right to a portion of the ashes of Gautama, were the Vajjis of Vaisâli. They are depicted[1] in early Buddhist sculptures as wearing Scythian garb. Whether Vajji is simply a variation of *Yue-chi*, and whether the Lichhavi clan, said to be an offshoot of the Vajji, are to be identified with the Litsavi, a Mongolo-Scythic tribe in Thibet, is uncertain, but probable. Another tribe, the Gandhâras, must have originally come from the distant North-West Frontier, where Scythians would naturally be found. If these two tribes were Scythian, the tribe of Gautama must have been Scythian too. And so, perhaps, we are justified in including Buddhism among the products of early foreign influence in India.

In 538 B.C., Cyrus the Great took Babylon by storm, and became Master of Western Asia—"King of Babel, Sumer, Akkad, and the four quarters of the world." Twenty years later, his equally great successor, Darius, crossed the Carmanian Desert to claim the allegiance of Eastern Iran. Darius was a splendid organizer and financier—his abilities in that latter direction had gained him the contemptuous title of Κάπηλος, "The Pedlar," from the Persian nobility,—and he was struck with the brilliant idea of annexing the Indus Valley to his eastern possessions. The scheme was carried out in a most

[1] Cunningham, *Anc. Geog. of India*, 447, Beal, in *J.R.A.S.*, xiv. 39.

methodical fashion: the Panjab was occupied, and an expedition was sent under a Greek named Scylax of Caryanda to explore the Indus Valley and to travel home by sea from the mouth of the river.[1] The explorers accomplished their task with complete success; they returned by the old route followed by Solomon's trading fleet, and landed eighteen months later near the modern port of Suez.

We know so little of the history of Persia, that there is not much to record of the "Satrapy of India" during the two centuries which preceded the invasion of Alexander. That the country fully realized the expectations of Darius is shown by the enormous tribute which it paid to the imperial coffers. Indian contingents fought in the Persian campaigns against Greece. Perhaps Taxila was the capital of the province, for Alexander's soldiers found there traces of Persian and Babylonian customs; the people held a marriage-market every year in their city, like the Babylonians, and exposed their dead for the vultures to devour instead of cremating them.[2] Darius was the first monarch to have both Greek and Indian subjects under his rule. Of the mainland of Greece,

[1] He started from an unidentified city called "Caspatyrus in Pactyica," somewhere in the North-West Panjab. Probably *Κασπάτυρος* is a misreading for *Κασπάπυρος* (Kaspa-pura), defined by Hecatæus as *Γανδαρικὴ πόλις Σκυθῶν ἀκτή*, "A city of Gandhâra on the Scythian border." Pactyica is the land of the Pachtu or Pashtu, the Pathans or Afghans.

[2] A Median custom, borrowed from the Scythians, who gave their dead to "dogs and birds" to devour. At Bactria, the home of Zoroastrianism, a special breed of dogs, called *ἐνταφιασταί*, "Entombers," were kept for the purpose. The Persians buried their dead. The tomb of Cyrus at Pasargadæ, for instance, is a proof of this.

India knew nothing; the Ionians of Asia Minor, employed in the Great King's service, or traders of the same nationality who put in at Barbarikon or Barygaza, were the only Greeks with whom they were acquainted. Hence we may dismiss at once any theories about the influence of Greek literature on India before Alexander's invasion. The Sanskrit *Yavana*, Ἰάϝων, dates from the time when the digamma was still in use. The Prakrit *Yôna*, Ἰων, is, of course, later.[1] There seems little doubt that the Persian occupation of the Panjab made a great impression upon India; Persian customs and Persian architecture were probably adopted at the courts of some of the local râjas. One unmistakable trace of Persian influence lasted in Western India for many centuries after the Persian Empire had disappeared. This was the Kharoshthi script, introduced by the officials of the Achæmenids, which was not entirely replaced by the Brâhmi writing till the fourth century A.D. The Kharoshthi is undoubtedly Aramaic in origin, reading, like other kindred scripts, from right to left.[2] The last hope of Persia perished with the gallant young Cyrus on the field of Cunaxa

[1] Compare Milton's "Ionian gods of Javan's issue held." *P.L.*, i. 508, and *S.A.*, 715-6. Milton got the word from Isa. lxvi. 19, but he mixes up Javan with Javan son of Japheth (Gen. x. 2). The Greeks heard of India from the Persians. Ἰνδοί is Hendu, the Avesta word, and not Sindava (Skt.). Otherwise we should have Ἵνδοι, as Max Müller points out. Hecatæus (520 B.C.) is the first to mention India among surviving Greek writers. Some of the stories in Herodotus—*e.g.* the story of Hippocleides—have been traced to India, through Persia. Tawney, *Journal of Philology*, xii. 112.

[2] A highly amusing article by Prof. Lacouperie, in the *Babylonian and Oriental Record*, 1886, p. 58, ascribes this script to Cyrus (Khusru). Unfortunately Cyrus never visited India.

(401 B.C.). After this the great Empire began to break up. Eastern Iran became a practically independent kingdom under the Satrap of Balkh, who was always a member of the Royal family. We cease to hear of Indian troops in the Persian army, and probably the annual Indian tribute seldom found its way to the Imperial coffers.

II

In 329 B.C. Alexander entered the Panjab. He found Western India governed by a number of independent princes, controlled by no sort of central government. In this disunited condition, they fell an easy prey to the Macedonian forces, in spite of the desperate resistance which was offered from time to time by the gallant natives. Alexander marched across the Panjab in a south-easterly direction to the river Bias, where he was compelled to turn back. He then retreated to the banks of the Jhilam, and sailed down that stream to its confluence with the Indus, and thence to the coast, subduing and organizing the country as he went. The conquered lands were put in charge of governors, native and Greek; elaborate arrangements were made for building a harbour at Pattala; Nearchus was sent to explore, and re-opened the old Phœnician trade route between the mouths of the Indus and Euphrates. Unfortunately, these far-seeing plans came to nothing. In 323 B.C., two years after leaving India, Alexander died. The empire collapsed like a pack of cards; at the same time a great national movement under Chandragupta united all Aryan India under a single leader, and the Macedonian governors were glad to hurry away to the further side of the Hindu Kush with such booty as they could lay hands on.

By 321 B.C., Macedonian power was at an end in India; only those settlers remained who cared to throw in their lot with the people.[1] The effect of the great invasion was practically *nil*, unless the example of Alexander inspired the enterprising Chandragupta with the idea of making himself master of Northern India.

We now come to the age of the enlightened and powerful Maurya dynasty, which may be compared with the age of the Antonines in Rome for wisdom, progress and moderation, though there is a certain spirituality about the great Asoka which is hardly found in Marcus Aurelius himself. It was a period of Renaissance in India: a great religious revival was accompanied by a magnificent artistic outburst. Shrines and palaces of stone suddenly replaced the wood and plaster erections of earlier days; clemency of a type unknown in India prevailed in the government; free communication with the hitherto despised "barbarian" was welcomed and encouraged. The difference which organization could make to a country's powers of resistance was seen when Seleucus Nicator tried in 305 B.C. to repeat the exploits of Alexander. The "Victorious" monarch quickly found it prudent to come to terms with his adversary. A friendly agreement was made, ceding a large portion of Eastern Iran to India, and the compact was sealed

[1] Quite possibly considerable Yavana colonies remained behind. They are mentioned in Asoka's inscriptions, and probably the king Apollodotus, whose coins are so difficult to place, belongs to this race, and not to the Bactrian dynasties.

by a marriage between Chandragupta and a Syrian princess. The relations between the Mauryas and their western neighbours was of the most cordial kind. Chandragupta was an enthusiastic admirer of Greek customs. Envoys from the West were in attendance at Pataliputra, and the presence of a Greek *râni* must have enhanced the philhellenic tendencies of the court. Among the ambassadors, the most famous was Megasthenes, the Syrian envoy to Chandragupta; in the reign of Bindusara he was succeeded by Deimachus. We also hear of a Dionysius from the court of Alexandria, who appears to have been in residence in the reign of Asoka.[1] A friendly and often amusing correspondence between the Maurya kings and their Syrian neighbours testifies to the intimate character of the relations between India and the Greek world at that time. Chandragupta sends Seleucus some powerful Indian drugs; Bindusara requests of Antiochus a consignment of "figs, Greek wine, and a sophist"; to which that monarch replies, that while delighted to send the wine, he regrets that it is not "good form for Greeks to deal in sophists" (οὐ νόμιμον ἐν Ἕλλησι σοφιστὴν πωλεῖσθαι). After his conversion to Buddhism, Asoka's first thought is for his friends, the Greek rulers of Syria and Alexandria. And yet, in spite of the intimacy between India and the West under the Mauryas, we can discern very few actual traces of Greek influence on Indian civilization during that period. The court of Chandragupta, as described by Megasthenes,[2] was conducted in Persian fashion. As in Persia, the king

[1] Strabo, 2, i, 9. Pliny, *N.H.* 17.
[2] V. A. Smith, *Early History of India*, ch. v.

lived in strict seclusion, and observed Persian festivals like the curious "hair-washing festival" held on the king's birthday.[1] Offences were punished by mutilation, a Persian practice abhorred by the Greeks. The country was split up into provinces, like the Persian satrapies. Asoka, when he determined to use a more lasting material than the wood and plaster of his predecessors for architectural purposes, set his workmen to erect buildings and monuments of stone in the Persian style, but adapted and Indianized in characteristic Hindu fashion. At the same time, we may discern traces of Scythian influence in the sculpture of the period. The grotesque, broad-shouldered figures of the Sanchi carvings are certainly not Aryan in type. The same type of figure appears even in the semi-Hellenic sculptures of the Gandhâra school.

We may take it for granted that the inhabitants of the Aryavarta at the time of the accession of Chandragupta were already a highly civilized people. No remains, alas, of the early architecture of India have survived, owing to the fragile nature of the materials employed, but we can see that the beautifully carved and inscribed pillars of Asoka are not the crude efforts of a primitive nation. At the same time, their essentially Indian appearance seems to prove that they are not the work of foreign artizans, like the Gandhâra sculptures. The numerous "sermons in stone" erected by Asoka, show that

[1] "A Royal Festival is held once a year on the birthday of Xerxes. It is called *Tycta* in Persian. The king washes his head and makes presents to the Persians." Herod. ix. 110.

"When the King (Chandragupta) washes his hair, they celebrate a great festival and send him presents." Strabo, xv. 69.

reading was a common accomplishment,[1] otherwise their erection all over the country would have been pointless. For two centuries constant intercourse with Persia, combined with the indigenous culture of the people, had produced an advanced civilization to which the rude Macedonian could add nothing, and upon which even Hellenistic refinement had comparatively little influence. Already, when Megasthenes arrived at Pataliputra, he found it as splendid as Susa or Ecbatana; and it was from Susa, *viâ* Taxila, that foreign influence had influenced the country. A Persian official, Tushâspa,[2] carried out Asoka's irrigation schemes in Kathiawar, doubtless on the model of the famous Babylonian works; the great trunk road, built from Pataliputra through Delhi to the North-West Frontier, was suggested, no doubt, by the Royal road of Darius in Persia.

A great deal has been made of the sudden introduction of stone as a building material by Asoka. It may be, of course, that he learnt from foreigners, perhaps Greeks, to use stone instead of wood. But it seems clear that he employed native craftsmen to work in this material, and allowed them to treat it very much in their own fashion. Thus any one examining

[1] The common legend that writing was not practised in India arose from the fact that most Sanskrit *literature* was transmitted orally, and legal disputes were settled by unwritten local custom. Strabo, xiv. 53, 67, etc. Writing was confined to secular purposes: even in the fifth century A.D. Fa Hian had the greatest difficulty in getting MSS. of Buddhist works. Perhaps Asoka borrowed from Persia the idea of inscribing long records upon the surface of rocks where they would meet the eye of the passer-by.

[2] Called, however, a *Yona*, in the Girnar Inscription. No doubt he spoke Greek. He may have been a Greek half-breed from Bactria.

the carvings of the Sanchi Stupi will recognize that the workmen employed were used to working in wood. The famous "Buddhist rail" at Sanchi is built of stone blocks elaborately hewn into the likeness of wooden logs, and a significant inscription records that one of the gates was the work of the "ivory carvers of Vidisa."[1] The truth is, that stone was not extensively used for building purposes till a much later period. Even four centuries later, Hiuen Tsiang regards the deserted ruins of Asoka's stone palaces with superstitious awe, as "the work of no mortal hands." Kanishka's great relic tower at Peshawar was of wood,[2] and wood was used for the fortifications of Pataliputra. The huge wooden arches in the Karla Caves show to what use wood could be put by Indian builders, and no doubt the vast majority of the buildings of the time were of wood and plaster, built on brick foundations, such as are still popular in Western India. Asoka's more ambitious schemes were partly due to religious enthusiasm, and partly, no doubt, to the great access of wealth which resulted from the excellent organization of his vast empire. Persian influence may be detected in the bell-shaped pillars and "lion-capitals" of the Buddhist architecture of the Maurya period, but it is so adapted and transformed that we cannot help tracing its first introduction back for many years before the accession of Chandragupta, to the time when the Persian, Indian, and Central Asian races first encountered one another in that strange meeting-place of nations, the Panjab.

[1] So, too, in the *Toy Cart*, the Palace has a "high ivory portal." V. A. Smith, *Hist. Fine Art*, x. 8.

[2] Beal, *Buddhist Records*, i. 103.

III

The "Yellow Peril" was no new thing to the ancient world. The Assyrian Empire had been menaced by the threats of Scythian incursions; and Scythians assisted at the sack of Nineveh. Cyrus the Great fell in battle against these traditional foes of the Aryan race, and Alexander, though compelled to destroy Cyropolis, the fortress built by the Persian monarch to guard the passage over the Jaxartes, replaced it by an even greater stronghold in the shape of Alexandria Eschaté. But the chief safeguard for the Aryans of Western Asia was the ancient Iranian province of Balkh or Bactria, the great buffer-state between the Persian Empire and the peoples of the steppes of Central Asia. Alexander had realized the strategic importance of Balkh to his eastern possessions, and had established there a large military colony. After his death this colony had grown into the dimensions of an important kingdom, the veterans having freely intermarried with the Iranian and Scythic populace. In 250 B.C. they revolted against the Syrian Empire, and their independence was recognized some forty years later by Antiochus the Great. That monarch had marched against the revolting province and laid siege to the capital, but he was induced to abandon his design by the plea that if he weakened this outpost of the Greek world, the Scythians would burst in and overrun the whole of the West at once.[1] Unfortunately, the Bactrians did not confine themselves to the *rôle* of guarding

[1] *ἐκβαρβαρωθήσεσθαι τὴν Ἑλλάδα ὁμολογουμένως.* Polyb. xi. 34.

the Oxus; the disorders which followed upon the break-up of the Maurya Empire, left the Panjab as a tempting prey to an ambitious conqueror, and the Bactrian monarchs were unable to resist the opportunity. About 190 B.C. the Bactrian king Demetrius invaded the north-west of India, and made himself master of a considerable portion of territory. This he made into a separate kingdom, with its capital at Sâgala,[1] which he renamed Euthydemeia after his father Euthydemus. This left Bactria proper in a precarious condition. Harassed by internal dissentions, and by continual quarrels with their old rivals the Parthians, the Bactrian Greeks could ill-afford to send the flower of their troops on distant expeditions to the far South. As Justin says, they were literally "drained of their life-blood."[2] In consequence, the Scythians at last managed to cross the Oxus, and overrun the country. Heliodorus, the last Greek king to reign north of the Hindu Kush, hastily evacuated Bactria, and fled, with such of his followers as did not care to submit to the invaders, to find a home in the province of Sâgala, which his predecessors had established. This was about 140 B.C. Unfortunately, the Greeks were continually quarrelling among themselves, and split up into a number of independent principalities. Only once, under the great Menander, did they unite for a brief time; and by 20 A.D. they disappeared altogether, though little isolated Greek states probably struggled on here and there till a much later period.[3]

[1] Probably Sialkot.

[2] *Exsangues.* Justin, xli. 6.

[3] Thus Gautamiputra (after 130 A.D.) talks of subduing Yavanas. (Rapson, *Coins of the Andras*, Section 44, Introduction.)

These Greeks had really very little Western blood in their veins when they settled in India, and their influence upon this country was very slight. They issued, however, some very beautiful and remarkable coins, one or two of which will compare with anything produced in the ancient world. It is impossible to explain this outburst of artistic genius in the furthest confines of Hellenic influence. These Bactrian coins were imitated extensively by the few Indian rulers who showed any taste in this direction, the Kushans, the Guptas, and the Western Kshatrapas, especially Nahapana, the ruler who issued the coins found in such immense numbers near Nasik, some years ago.[1] The Greek word *drachma* has passed into the vernacular language of to-day: from it came the Prakrit *dramma* and the modern *dâm*.[2] Otherwise it appears that the Greeks were rapidly absorbed in the native population. The process may be traced in the coinage, where Indian figures and inscriptions replace by degrees the Greek types of the earlier monarchs, and the workmanship becomes more and more debased. The few remains we have of the Indo-Greeks seem to show that they quickly lost all traces of their individuality, and adopted the religion, and even in many cases the names, of their neighbours. Thus the Karla Caves contain many inscriptions recording donations from the "Yavanas." These must be Bactrian Greeks; but they have Hindu names, and are Buddhists. The pillar recently discovered at

[1] See the *Journal B.B.R.A.S.*, vol. xxii. 224.

[2] The Kushans and Guptas also imitated extensively the Roman coins which poured into India in the first and second centuries A.D. *Dînar* is the Roman *Denarius*.

Besnagar[1] bears an inscription to the effect that it is the work of "Heliodorus, a worshipper of Krishna, sent by the Yona King Antialcidas." The pillar is in the Indo-Persian style, and contains no traces of Greek workmanship. Probably the Greek language was only used at the court of Sâgala, and among a few of the ruling class who had not intermarried with the natives. The Indo-Greek kingdoms reached the height of their power under the Buddhist prince Menander, who for a brief space carried the Greek arms to the walls of Pataliputra. Of his court and capital we find a delightful picture in the Buddhist *Questions of Milinda*,[2] which describes them as follows:

"There is in the country of the Yonakas a great centre of trade, a city called Sâgala. . . . Wise architects have laid it out, and its people know of no oppression, since all their enemies and adversaries have been put down. Brave is its defence, with many and strong towers and ramparts, with superb gates and entrance archways; and with the royal citadel in its midst, white-walled and deeply moated. Well laid out are its streets, squares, cross-roads, and market-places. Well displayed are the innumerable sorts of costly merchandise with which its shops are filled. It is richly adorned with hundreds of almshalls of various kinds, and splendid with hundreds of thousands of magnificent mansions, which rise aloft like the mountain-peaks of the

[1] *J.R.A.S.*, 1909, p. 1092.

[2] *S.B.E.* xxv. The book is so replete with detail that it must have been written soon after the time of Menander, by one who knew the country.

Himalayas. Its streets are filled with elephants, horses, carriages, frequented by men of all sorts and conditions—Brahmins, nobles, artificers, and servants. They resound with cries of welcome to the teachers of every creed, and the city is the resort of the leading men of each of the differing sects." In the unoppressive government, the white-walled acropolis, and the "welcome given to teachers of every sect,"[1] we may perhaps discern echoes of the old Greek spirit; but Menander was essentially an Indian raja, and not a Greek ruler. A Siamese tradition affirms that he took the yellow robe in his old age, and died an *arhat;* and Plutarch relates a story[2] to the effect that at his funeral, as at that of Gautama Buddha, seven nations disputed for a share of his ashes, which they carried away and buried beneath *stûpas* (μνήμεια) in their own countries. As far as we can tell at present, the Indo-Greeks exercised very little intellectual influence upon India, though excavation on the site of the ancient Sâgala may modify this view. If, however, Menander used the same flimsy materials for his great palaces and fortresses as his Indian contemporaries, not much remains to be unearthed.

In the meanwhile, bodies of Sakas were beginning to appear in the Panjab and to settle in the vicinity of Taxila, Mathura, and other places. One isolated tribe eventually reached Kathiawar.[3] Great numbers somewhere about this time flocked into the modern

[1] Cf. Acts of the Apostles xvii. 21.

[2] In the tract *Reip. Gerend.* p. 121.

[3] The modern Jats are perhaps descendants of the famous Scythian tribe, the Getæ.

Sistan (Sakastan), giving the country its modern name. These immigrants appear to have been accompanied by a certain number of Parthians, but in spite of the ingenuity of modern numismatologists, very little can be said with certainty about these petty chieftains. Whether there was an actual Parthian invasion of the Panjab is unknown, and, after all, not very important; but coins and inscriptions show that a powerful Saka dynasty was succeeded by a line of monarchs bearing Parthian names, who employed satraps to govern the more distant parts of their realms. The Greeks, who were continually quarrelling among themselves, could offer no resistance to these new-comers. Hindu writers speak contemptuously of the "Sakas, Yavanas, and Pahlavas," as a set of barbarians with little to distinguish them. There is little doubt that the sudden incursion of Saka tribes was caused by pressure from the North. After a series of obscure movements, a powerful Mongolian tribe called the Yueh-chi had treated the Sakas of Bactria precisely as the latter had formerly treated the Bactrian Greeks, and thus the Sakas were in their turn compelled to seek new homes south of the Hindu Kush. In the meanwhile, the nomads who now held Bactria, settled down in that fertile country and rapidly became a powerful and civilized nation. In their new abode they acquired a certain amount of culture; from the remnants of the Scythian and Iranian peoples of Balkh they adopted a debased form of Zoroastrianism; while from the Greeks of the country, or perhaps the Parthians, they took over the Greek alphabet, and possibly a certain modicum of the Greek language. Finally, about the first century A.D., the Yueh-chi began, like their predecessors, to cast envious eyes upon the Panjab, and a Yueh-chi monarch named Kadphises, belonging to the dominant Kushan clan, quietly overran the decadent Indo-Greek and Saka principalities in North-Western India.[1] That the Greeks submitted without a struggle appears from the fact that the last Greek prince, Hermæus, issued coins in conjunction with Kadphises until his death, when Kadphises appears alone. The Kushans rapidly made themselves masters of Northern India. Kanishka, their most powerful prince, must have ruled from the Jaxartes to the mouth of the Ganges. He appears to have sent an embassy to the Emperor Trajan, and for the next two centuries the trade between Rome and India reached very large dimensions. Some idea of the extent of the commerce between the two countries may be gathered from the immense finds of Roman coins which have been made from time to time in India. Five cooly loads of *aurei* of the reign of Nero were found some years ago near Cannanore, and this is by no means an isolated instance.[2] Pliny complains bitterly of the "drain"

[1] The invasion was no doubt quite a peaceful one; the "Kshatrapas" merely acknowledged their new overlords and remained undisturbed.

[2] An immense amount of trade passed between India and the West in the first century B.C. It was stimulated by Augustus' suppression of piracy, and by the discovery of the monsoon by Hippalus, c. 48 A.D. The goods were sent to Myos Hormus on the Red Sea, and transhipped at Alexandria. Strabo saw 120 ships leave Myos Hormus for India. The chief port was Muziris (probably Mangalore), and it was a run of only forty days from Aden to that port in the monsoon. Indian Rajas often had Greek bodyguards, and Greek girls in their harems. The Greek janissary was useful because he could form no plots, being ignorant of the language of the country. *Yavana* hence, like *Suisse* in the

caused by the shipment of Roman gold and silver to India in return for useless and unproductive luxuries, and anticipates the gravest results therefrom.[1] Perhaps this export of Roman money really had something to do with the disastrous financial paralysis which finally overtook the Roman Empire. Similar complaints about the absorption of money by India are not unknown in modern times, the Kushans, having no indigenous culture of their own, were forced, as they became a settled nation, to borrow from their neighbours. The result, as seen in their coins, is a curious medley. From the Parthians they took over the titles of *Kshatrapa*, *King of Kings*, etc., probably because no change in the government of the subordinate provinces was made when they conquered the country. From the Parthians, too, they borrowed the Greek script generally in vogue, modifying it, however, to express certain sounds not known to the Greek tongue. Thus P on the Kushan coins represents not *r* but *sh*; KOPANO KANEPKI is "Kanishka the Kushan," and the title PAONANO is the Pahlava *Shahan-shah*, *βασιλεὺς βασίλεων*.[2] It does not follow, of course, that the Kushans spoke Greek because they employed the Greek script. The Greek script is frequently

eighteenth century, comes to be used very vaguely. Nowadays it means any Westerner, even a Mahommedan. So *Roumi* among the Turks and Arabs.

[1] "Minima computatione milies centena milia sestertium annis omnibus India et Seres peninsulaque illa imperio nostro adimunt." *N.H.* 12. 18.

[2] For the whole question, see Stein's *Zoroastrian Deities on Indo-Scythian Coins.* (Babylonian and Oriental Record, vol. i. p. 133.) Perhaps in this letter we have a revival of the Σάν, the Indian S', used at one time by the Dorians. It may have survived in a remote corner of the Greek world.

used by various rulers of the time, indifferently with the Brahmi or Kharoshthi, to express Prakrit coin-legends. A curious example of the confusion of Greek and Indian ideas by these semi-barbarous tribes is a coin of Kanishka bearing a *male* figure of the moon, and inscribed ΣΑΛΗΝΗ.[1] The Goddess NANAIA appears on many Kushan coins. She is the Zoroastrian Anaitis, the tutelary deity of Balkh, and it appears probable that she and many other Zoroastrian deities,[2] were imported by the Kushans from their ancient home on the Oxus. In some cases, no doubt, the Kushans merely continued the local coins of the districts over which they ruled, and it is possible that the Zoroastrian coins of the Kushans were issued for circulation in Pahlava settlements and satrapies. The deity on a particular coin very often represents the religion, not of the king who strikes it, but of the district for use in which it is minted.

Far more important, however, was the importation by Kanishka of Greek artists from Asia Minor to decorate the numerous shrines, monasteries, and other buildings with which, in the first enthusiasm of his conversion to the Buddhist creed, he covered the district round his capital town, Peshawar. The productions of these workmen and their Indian imitators still cover the ancient country of Gandhâra in vast quantities, and their influence upon Buddhist art was very considerable. It is a curious thing that it was left to a Scythian, and not to the Indo-Greeks, to introduce Hellenic art into India. Of the artistic value of the "Gandhâra School" of sculpture, very

[1] B. M. Cat. xxvi. 1. [2] Also represented on Kushan coins.

varying estimates have been formed. Many Europeans, educated on Greek models, have found them more familiar and intelligible than the purely Hindu work of the following period, and have, in consequence lavished upon them a quite disproportionate amount of praise. On the other hand, the recent school of Indian critics, which has done so much for ancient Hindu art, condemns them as utterly worthless attempts on the part of fifth-rate Hellenistic workmen to represent subjects they do not in the least comprehend. This, I think, is a little exaggerated. No one in his senses would compare the work of Kanishka's semi-barbarous Indo-Scythian mechanics, or the decadent Syrian sculptors imported from Ephesus and Pergamum, with the Elephanta bas-reliefs, or the magnificent Mahâyâna Buddhist statues of Java, or the South Indian bronzes. They are obviously second-rate; they are not even up to the average standard of the Hellenistic art of the period. They are evidently "made to order," and show comparatively few traces of higher artistic feeling. It is, after all, impossible for any one to represent purely Eastern ideas by Western methods. The result is always lamentable.[1] On the other hand, we could ill-afford to lose these interesting, realistic, and often pretty representatives of Indian life in the first century A.D.[2] To the student of Buddhism they are a mine of information, an entrancing record of the beliefs of the time. We should beware of under-estimating their value and interest. Their importance, too, in

[1] Take, for instance, the atrocities of Ravi Varma, unhappily so popular in Western India.

[2] See the Indo-Greek Buddha, for instance, on p. 5.

the history of Buddhist art is very great. The Greeks first taught the Indians to represent the Master in human form; it is possible that they are responsible for the introduction of sculptured representations of the gods of the Hindu Pantheon as well. The conventional Buddha of modern Buddhism originated from the Gandhâra sculptures. Buddhism has now become very largely the religion of the Mongolian nations, and the modern type of the Buddha has Mongolian features; but in the hair, the halo, and the arrangement of the drapery, we may discern clear traces of his Indo-Greek origin. The Gandhâra school, no doubt, influenced the Far East through Khotan, where abundant remains of semi-Mongolian culture, strongly tinged by Indo-Greek ideas, have recently been discovered. The amount of Hellenistic influence in the Gandhâra sculptures varies considerably. Some of the statues and bas-reliefs are obviously the work of Greek artists; Zeus does duty as Kubera, Pallas Athene as an Indian attendant. Purely Greek themes like Hercules and the Lion, Ganymede and the Eagle, Tritons, Centaurs, and so forth, are reproduced with no attempt at concealment. Others, again, are much less Greek, both in type and subject. They represent scenes from the Jâtaka Stories, treated with a humorous realism which takes us back to the older Maurya sculptures. The short, broad-shouldered figures appearing in these sculptures are Scythian rather than Aryan. Probably they were the work of native craftsmen working under Greek overseers. In the later remains of the period, we find debased Corinthian pillars, bearing figures in the foliage, which are Roman rather than Greek. Some of them are "finished" with stucco in a similar fashion to the pillars of the Baths of Caracalla (217 A.D.).[1] As we have already mentioned, there was a considerable intercourse between Rome and India in the first three centuries after Christ.

The most unpleasing remains of the period are the repulsive Mathura sculptures, which probably belong to a local Tantric cult, as Mr. Vincent Smith supposes. The finest work of the time, on the other hand, is found at Amrâvati. The Amrâvati bas-reliefs show very little Greek influence, having been executed under the orders of the Andra princes, who were not, like the Kushans, foreigners without a culture of their own. On the whole, the influence of Greece on the Gandhâra and kindred schools of culture has been exaggerated; we may find a good many traces in Kushan art of the ancient traditions of the Maurya period, partly Indo-Persian, and partly Central Asian. The critics who are determined to find an origin for every striking artistic type, trace to Alexandria the practice of executing long bas-reliefs of an anecdotal character; in that case we must, perhaps, look for Greek influence, transmitted from Western India, in the wonderful mural sculptures of Java as well as in the Gandhâra friezes.

[1] These pillars are ornamental and not structural. The *buildings* erected by Kanishka must have been of the conventional Indian type, and to judge from the way in which they have disappeared, must have been mostly of wood and brick. It should be mentioned, by the way, that faint traces of Hellenistic influence before the Kushan era may be found, notably in the coins and other remains of Azes, and other Saka and Indo-Parthian rulers. Mention should also be made of the wonderful vase containing the Buddha relics, discovered in 1909, at Peshawar. It was the work of "Agesilaus, a workman of Kanishka."—*J.R.A.S.*, 1909, p. 1058.

IV

After the collapse of the Kushan Empire, attention reverts to Eastern India, where the great indigenous dynasty of the Guptas arose about 300 A.D. With the Gupta monarchs India begins once more to discard foreign influence; Buddhism, the creed of the cosmopolitan settlers of the Panjab, is slowly replaced by the more conservative Brahmanism; a great revival of Sanskrit literature takes place. In art, a very noticeable change is observed, both in style and subject. The short, broad-shouldered type of figure gives place to the long-limbed, graceful forms which are characteristic of later Hindu art. Hindu subjects replace Buddhist ones. Did even this great conservative reaction owe anything to Western influence? The Guptas, while adhering strictly to national ideals, were a singularly enlightened dynasty. They encouraged foreign trade, and, like the Kushans, issued a gold coin in imitation of the Roman *aureus*. Indian philosophy began to make itself felt in the West; Neo-platonism undoubtedly bears traces of contact with Eastern ideas. Even Christianity borrowed something in the course of its development from Buddhism; relic-worship and monasticism found their way into the Church from the East; and Gautama Buddha, under the title of St. Josaphat, is still, *mirabile dictu*, recognized as a Christian saint. On the other hand, the East borrowed something in her turn from Western schools. Astronomy, which has a ritual as well as a scientific importance in India, was about this time very largely re-modelled upon the lines suggested by the researches of the Alexandrian mathematicians. Indians were quite frank about their indebtedness to Greece in this respect. "The Yavanas are indeed barbarians," says the *Gargi Samhita*, "but astronomy originated with them, and for this they must be venerated as gods." Of the five *siddhântas*, or astronomical systems, two, the *Rômaka siddhânta* and the *Paulisa Siddhânta* (the latter is named after Paul of Alexandria, *c.* 387 A.D.), are manifestly Western in origin. The word *jâmitra*, used by Kâlîdâsa (*Kumârasambhâva*, vii. 1), is the Greek διάμετρον.[1] Many of the names of the planets, as well as of the signs of the zodiac, are derived from the Greek.[2] Hindu medical science, in a similar fashion, is said to show distinct traces of Western influence, though this may have been introduced in Kushan times.[3]

We now come to a much more disputed question. Does the Indian drama, which reached its height of perfection under the Guptas, owe anything to Greece? If the Greek language was ever known to any extent in India, it would be easy to suppose that the Indian dramatists had read Menander and the other Greek writers. But can we infer this from the actual evidence which we have? A corrupt Greek was no doubt spoken at the Court of Sâgala by the successors of the Bactrian Greeks, but the coins show that it

[1] It is the seventh place on the horoscope, by which the astrologer predicts the happiness of married life for a person.

[2] *Vide* Dr. Vogel's article in *East and West*, Jan. 1912.

[3] Dr Vogel finds in the works of Charaka, "said to have been Kanishka's physician," very strong traces of a knowledge of Hippocrates.

was in a moribund condition.[1] Still more corrupt, if we may judge from the coins, was the Greek in use at the court of the Kushans; indeed, it is doubtful whether it was used at all, except for intercourse with foreigners, as the language of diplomacy and commerce. Traders at Barygaza must have picked up a little of the language, and so must the stonemasons who associated with Kanishka's foreign workmen. But this does not imply a knowledge of the literary, written language of classical Greece. Nor can we rely much upon the fact that Indian astronomers and doctors were acquainted with Greek astronomy and medicine. The knowledge was brought to India by students who had studied abroad. In the same way, medieval Europe owed a great deal to Arabian astronomers and scientists, but this does not imply that Roger Bacon or other students knew Arabic. As a matter of fact, we know they did not.

Only one Indian play, the *Toy Cart*, shows any real resemblance to a Greek comedy. Even Mr. Vincent Smith would hesitate to find likenesses in *Shakuntala* to any classical drama. Indeed, we might very well show the futility of making too much of such resemblances by comparing the Indian and Elizabethan dramas.[2] The Fool (*Vidus'aka*) certainly plays a prominent part in the plays of Shakespeare; *Shakuntala* resembles far more closely romantic comedies like the *Winter's Tale*, or the plays of

[1] It has even been held that the corrupt Greek inscriptions on Kushan and other coins are survivals of a dead language, like the Latin ones on our own coins.

[2] Dean Milman, in an article in the *Quarterly* for 1831, compared the Indian and Spanish dramas.

Beaumont and Fletcher, than any Greek drama. Then, again, Greek plays were acted in public, open-air theatres; Indian and Elizabethan plays in halls and courtyards. The small amphitheatre discovered by Dr. Bloch at Râmgarh[1] is unique, and may be, like the *Yavanikâ*, or Greek curtain,[2] the work of an ingenious Greek workman in Indian employ. Indian, like Elizabethan playwrights, show a sublime disregard for the unities, and mingle prose and verse indiscriminately. The *Nâtya S'âstra* of Bhârata, it is true, lays down a rule limiting the number of the persons appearing upon the stage to five, and the Sanskrit, like the classical drama, avoids the representation of violent or unseemly actions. But these conventions may very well have arisen independently. It is possible, of course, that the author of the *Nâtya S'âstra*, like the Indian writers on astronomy and medicine, *may* have derived some of his rules from Alexandria. The writer of the *Toy Cart may* have witnessed or read a Greek comedy. But the ingenious arguments of Weber and Windisch are merely clever special pleading; there is really no reason why the Indian drama should not have arisen, like the Greek, from primitive religious celebrations, quite independently of foreign influence. Mr. Vincent Smith, who is always anxious to deprive India of the credit of all her achievements in Art and Literature, thinks there is sufficient evidence to warrant our believing that Kâlîdâsa could read, not only Menander, but Terence! He also finds Greek influence in the typically Indian

[1] *Arch. Survey of India*, 1903–4, p. 123.

[2] *No* curtain was used on the Greek stage, hence this apparatus was *not* imported from Greece. Dr. Rapson says *Yavanikâ* merely means "made of Greek (or Western) material."

sculptures of the Gupta period.[1] The rhetorical statements of writers like Clement of Alexandria and Aelian, that there were Hindus who knew Homer and the Greek tragedians, need not be taken seriously. They probably arose from vague stories of the purely fortuitous points of resemblance between the Greek and Indian Epics.[2]

After 400 A.D., the Western world, in the throes of her last struggles with the barbarian, ceased to have commerce with the East, and India remained a vaguely known and legendary land to Europe until it was rediscovered by Vasco de Gama. The results arrived at in this essay are mainly negative; for the duty of the historian is, I conceive, to overthrow groundless assumptions and hasty conclusions before building up theories of his own. I hope I may have succeeded in showing how unjust are the theories which attribute any lasting influence upon India to Greece. To sum up, we may trace three distinct currents of foreign influence in India. Firstly, the influence of Babylon and Chaldea, which is visible in early Indian weights and measures and computations of time; secondly, Persian influence, which is very apparent in the court of the Mauryas; and, thirdly, Greco-Roman influence. This last dates from the time of the Kushan kings only (the Macedonian and Bactrian Greeks exerted no influence worth mentioning), and is to be seen in the Indo-Greek school of sculpture found in North-Western

[1] *Hist. Fine Art*, vi. 1.

[2] Like the supposed resemblance between the *Râmâyana* (the story of Sita) and the *Iliad* (the story of Helen) of which Weber absurdly makes so much.

India, in coinage, and in works on technical subjects, such as astronomy and medicine. It did not affect the literature. On the other hand, India influenced the West very considerably, from the time of the Phœnician traders to the adoption of certain Indian philosophical ideas and religious customs by Greeks and Christian thinkers. The latter question, however, has not yet been fully investigated: it awaits unbiassed and patient research.[1]

[1] It would be interesting to deal with the influence of India through Alexandria upon the early Christian Church. Monasticism and relic-worship may have been borrowed from Buddhism. Then we may ask whether Christ Himself owed any of His teaching to the Essenes, and they to the Buddhists of Balkh and Persia? Eastern thought influenced Neo-Platonism and Gnosticism, and possibly Origen. Saint Josaphat, Prince of India, still regarded as a saint by the Roman Church, reached Europe from Antioch. The presence of Indian fables in the *Gesta Romanorum*, Boccaccio, and in Chaucer is also a remarkable fact. See, for instance, Tawney's remarks in the *Journal of Philology*, vol. xii. pp. 112 and 203*ff*.

THE END

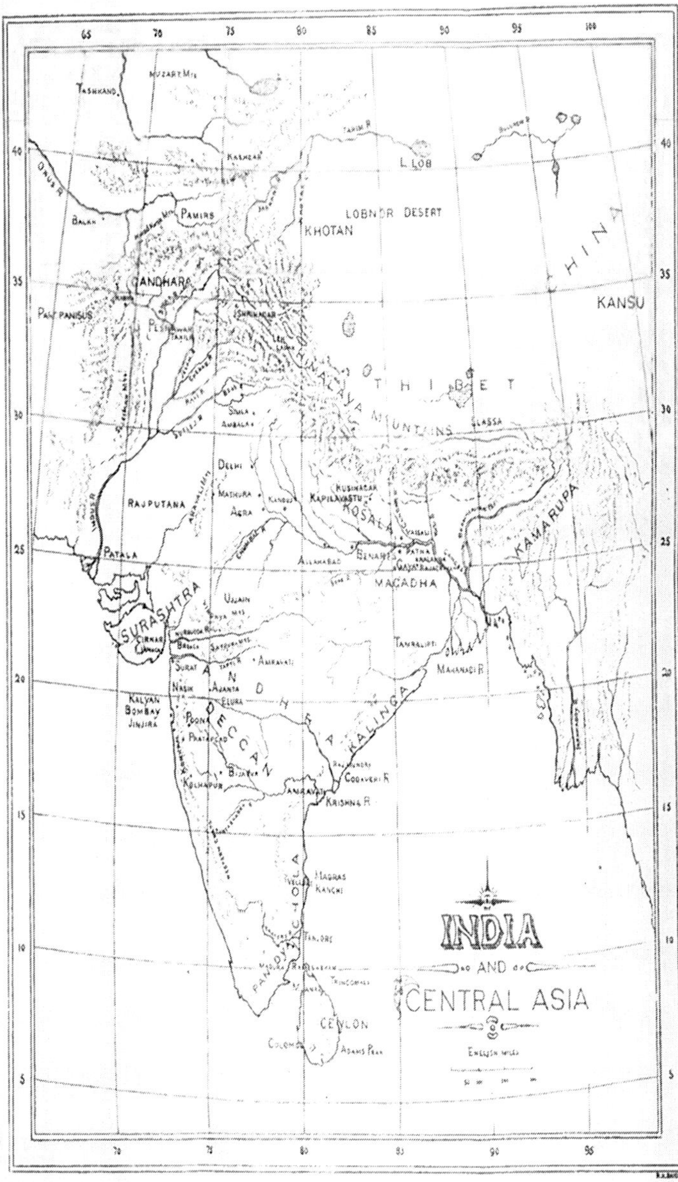

[At end of book.